HOW NEARLY EVERYTHING WAS INVENTED

by the Brainwaves

Illustrated by Lisa Swerling and Ralph Lazar

Written by Jilly MacLeod

CONTENTS

It's a really great book

Fantastic!

Stupendous!

You won't be able to put it down!

DK

LONDON, NEW YORK, MELBOURNE, MUNICH, and DELHI

Editor Niki Foreman
Designer Jim Green

Managing Editor Linda Esposito
Managing Art Editor Diane Thistlethwaite

Consultant Roger Bridgman

Jacket Copywriter Adam Powley
Jacket Editor Mariza O'Keeffe
Index John Noble

Publishing Managers Andrew Macintyre, Caroline Buckingham

Category Publisher Laura Buller

DTP Co-ordinator Siu Chan
Production Katherine Thornton

First published in Great Britain in 2006
by Dorling Kindersley Limited,
80 Strand, London WC2R 0RL

Copyright © 2006 Dorling Kindersley Limited
A Penguin Company
2 4 6 8 10 9 7 5 3 1

A CIP catalogue record for this book is available from the British Library.

ISBN-13: 978 1 40531 329 2
ISBN-10: 1 4053 1329 3

Colour reproduction by Icon Reproduction, UK

Printed and bound by Hung Hing, China

Discover more at
www.dk.com
www.thebrainwaves.com

About this book

Featuring the brainwaves – little people with big ideas – this fascinating book takes a light-hearted look at some of the world's most important inventions. The emphasis is on the consequences of invention, and how one idea leads to another. A key feature is the six double gatefolds, each of which focuses on a major invention – the lens, steam engine, light bulb, internal combustion engine, transistor, and gunpowder – exploring the inventions that preceded it and how it inspired the development of other inventions. In addition, there are special features, including the people behind the big ideas, classic failures, and what the future holds in store.

Special "How Things Work" boxes give step-by-step explanations

Portraits introduce the inventors

Timeline charts the development of a classic invention

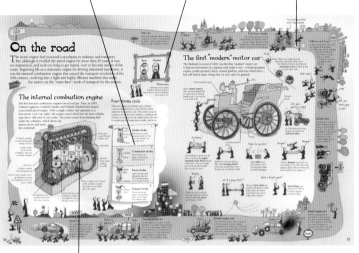

Cutaway diagram shows how it works

Introduction

The top two pages of each gatefold introduce a key invention, and explore a classic consequence of that invention (for example, the history of the car can be traced back to the development of the internal combustion engine).

Signposts direct you through the landscape

Discover how one idea led to another

Key invention is placed in the historical context of what came before and after

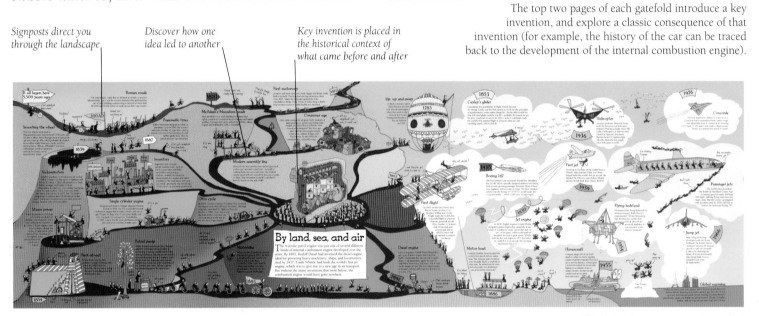

Folded-out gatefold

The gatefold folds out to reveal the key invention at the centre of a web of associated inventions, showing what preceded and succeeded the key invention and how all these ideas interrelate.

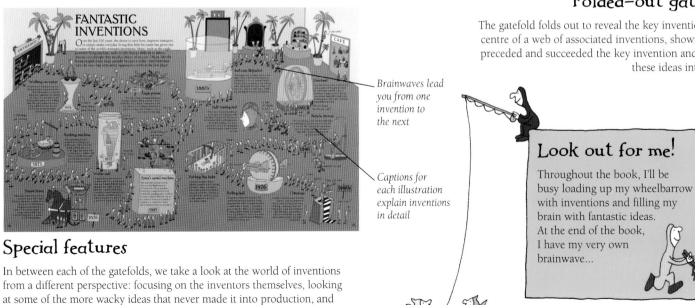

Brainwaves lead you from one invention to the next

Captions for each illustration explain inventions in detail

Special features

In between each of the gatefolds, we take a look at the world of inventions from a different perspective: focusing on the inventors themselves, looking at some of the more wacky ideas that never made it into production, and anticipating those that haven't even made it off the drawing board yet.

Look out for me!

Throughout the book, I'll be busy loading up my wheelbarrow with inventions and filling my brain with fantastic ideas. At the end of the book, I have my very own brainwave...

Finding a better way

Since people first roamed the planet more than a million years ago, the conviction that "there must be a better way than this" has inspired them to invent things. Some inventions are the brainchild of an individual working alone, while others are the result of teamwork. Many evolved over long periods of time, with numerous people taking a hand in their development; others were conceived within days. However they came about, one thing's for certain – without inventions we would all still be living in caves!

Printing changed the world

Strong wooden frame to withstand pressure of printing

Frisket folded down to hold paper in place on tympan

Ink used to coat type

Platen presses paper down onto type

Bar for screwing platen down

Printing paper placed on tympan

Tympan, with frisket holding paper in place, is folded down onto inked type

Rounce used to crank paper and type underneath platen

Type placed here, then inked

Early inventions

The world's earliest inventions were simple tools made by chipping away at lumps of stone to create a sharp cutting edge. These "handaxes" were used to butcher meat, prepare hides, and cut branches. They served their purpose for more than a million years until someone had the bright idea of adding a handle to improve the swing, and the axe was born!

I'm just protecting my patent

Aaargh!

Sharp idea!

It's the cutting edge of design

Inventions that changed the world

Some inventions have such a big impact on society that they change the world. One such invention was the method of printing developed in Germany by Johannes Gutenberg in about 1455. Before this, books were laboriously copied out by hand and were the sole preserve of churchmen, scholars, and kings. Afterwards, books could be mass-produced and new ideas shared by anyone who could read. Things would never be the same again!

Don't believe everything you read

Alpha foxtrot Iggy iggy tango Dot dot dash

It's either gibberish, martian, or some sort of secret code

Patent protection

Patents were developed in the 15th century to give inventors legal protection against people stealing their ideas and making money from them. To get a patent, an invention has to differ significantly from similar ideas. In the 19th century, for example, hundreds of patents were granted for barbed wire, each one for a different design.

Codes and languages

Some people are famous for inventing codes and languages rather than devices. Samuel Morse is best known for his Morse code, a dot-and-dash code that was once widely used to send telegraph messages. Computer pioneer Grace Hopper, on the other hand, invented a new language called COBOL that transformed the way computers were programmed.

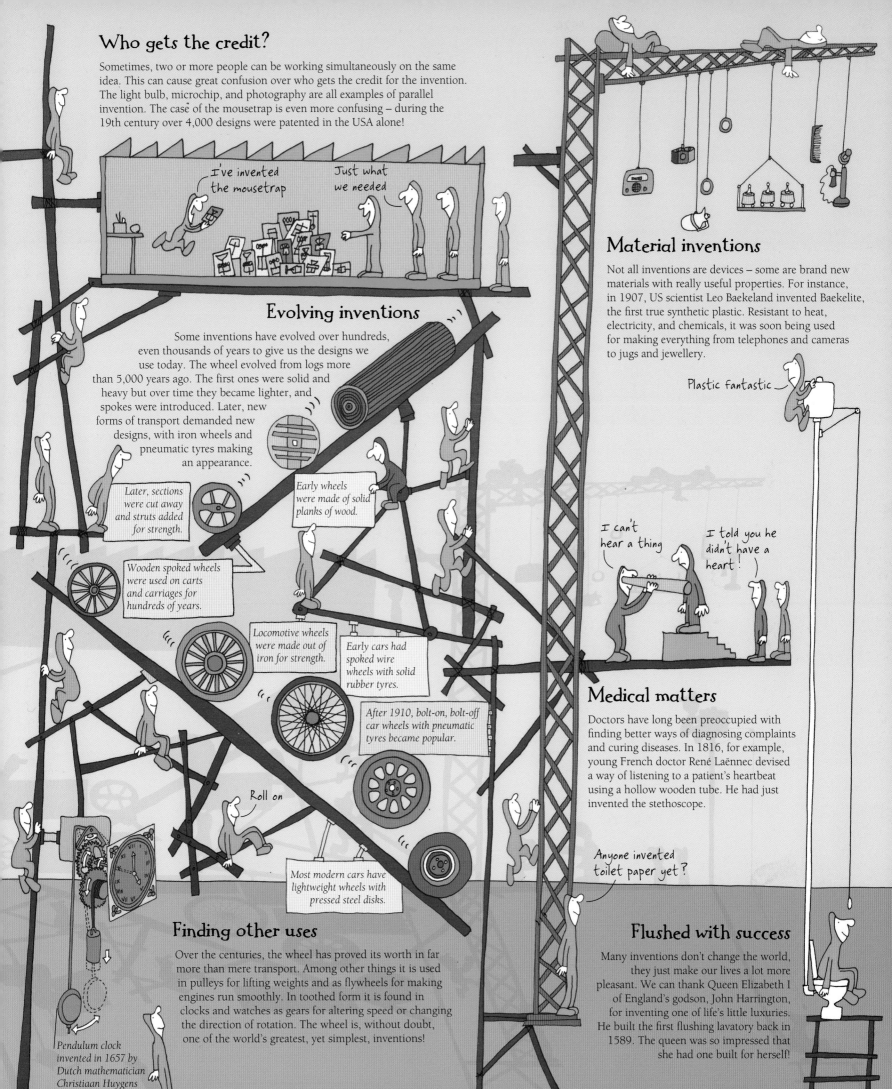

Who gets the credit?

Sometimes, two or more people can be working simultaneously on the same idea. This can cause great confusion over who gets the credit for the invention. The light bulb, microchip, and photography are all examples of parallel invention. The case of the mousetrap is even more confusing – during the 19th century over 4,000 designs were patented in the USA alone!

I've invented the mousetrap

Just what we needed

Evolving inventions

Some inventions have evolved over hundreds, even thousands of years to give us the designs we use today. The wheel evolved from logs more than 5,000 years ago. The first ones were solid and heavy but over time they became lighter, and spokes were introduced. Later, new forms of transport demanded new designs, with iron wheels and pneumatic tyres making an appearance.

Later, sections were cut away and struts added for strength.

Early wheels were made of solid planks of wood.

Wooden spoked wheels were used on carts and carriages for hundreds of years.

Locomotive wheels were made out of iron for strength.

Early cars had spoked wire wheels with solid rubber tyres.

After 1910, bolt-on, bolt-off car wheels with pneumatic tyres became popular.

Roll on

Most modern cars have lightweight wheels with pressed steel disks.

Finding other uses

Over the centuries, the wheel has proved its worth in far more than mere transport. Among other things it is used in pulleys for lifting weights and as flywheels for making engines run smoothly. In toothed form it is found in clocks and watches as gears for altering speed or changing the direction of rotation. The wheel is, without doubt, one of the world's greatest, yet simplest, inventions!

Pendulum clock invented in 1657 by Dutch mathematician Christiaan Huygens

Material inventions

Not all inventions are devices – some are brand new materials with really useful properties. For instance, in 1907, US scientist Leo Baekeland invented Baekelite, the first true synthetic plastic. Resistant to heat, electricity, and chemicals, it was soon being used for making everything from telephones and cameras to jugs and jewellery.

Plastic fantastic

I can't hear a thing

I told you he didn't have a heart!

Medical matters

Doctors have long been preoccupied with finding better ways of diagnosing complaints and curing diseases. In 1816, for example, young French doctor René Laënnec devised a way of listening to a patient's heartbeat using a hollow wooden tube. He had just invented the stethoscope.

Anyone invented toilet paper yet?

Flushed with success

Many inventions don't change the world, they just make our lives a lot more pleasant. We can thank Queen Elizabeth I of England's godson, John Harrington, for inventing one of life's little luxuries. He built the first flushing lavatory back in 1589. The queen was so impressed that she had one built for herself!

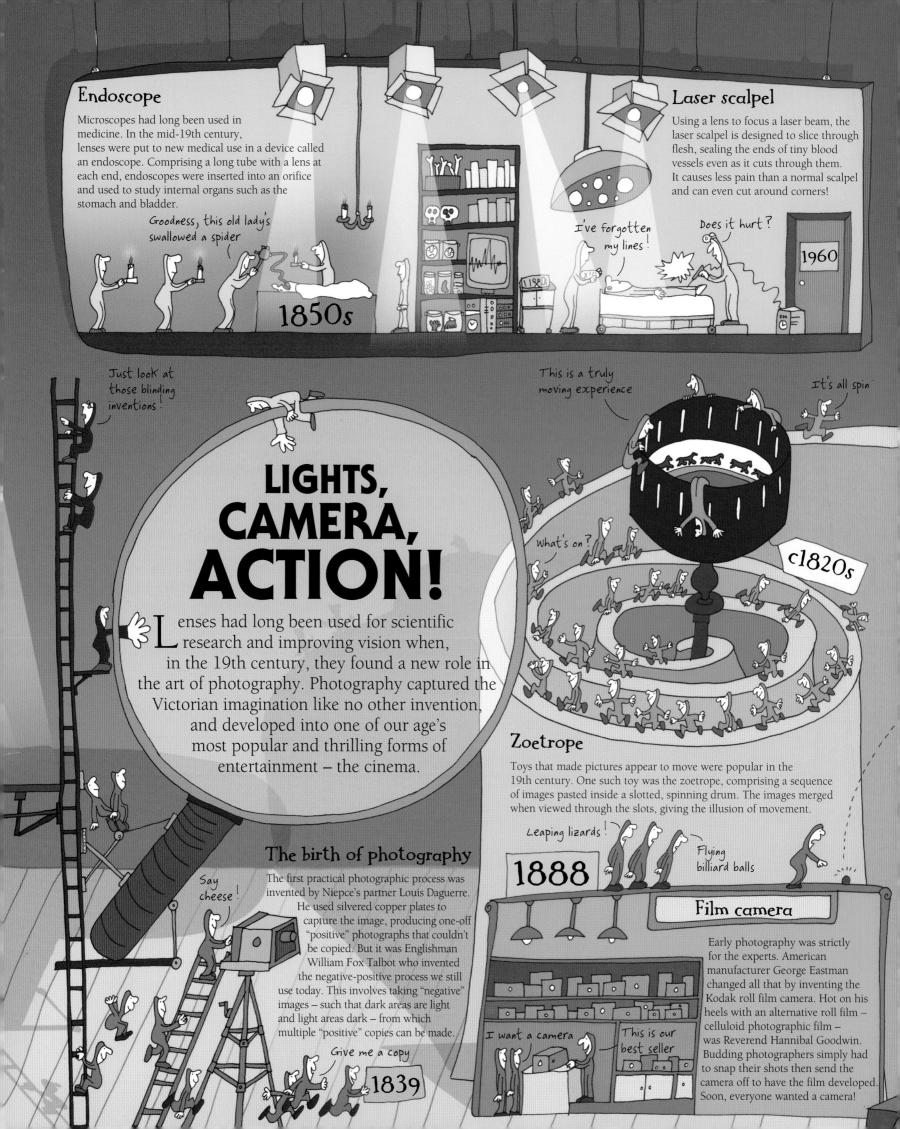

Endoscope

Microscopes had long been used in medicine. In the mid-19th century, lenses were put to new medical use in a device called an endoscope. Comprising a long tube with a lens at each end, endoscopes were inserted into an orifice and used to study internal organs such as the stomach and bladder.

1850s

Laser scalpel

Using a lens to focus a laser beam, the laser scalpel is designed to slice through flesh, sealing the ends of tiny blood vessels even as it cuts through them. It causes less pain than a normal scalpel and can even cut around corners!

1960

LIGHTS, CAMERA, ACTION!

Lenses had long been used for scientific research and improving vision when, in the 19th century, they found a new role in the art of photography. Photography captured the Victorian imagination like no other invention, and developed into one of our age's most popular and thrilling forms of entertainment – the cinema.

Zoetrope

Toys that made pictures appear to move were popular in the 19th century. One such toy was the zoetrope, comprising a sequence of images pasted inside a slotted, spinning drum. The images merged when viewed through the slots, giving the illusion of movement.

c1820s

1888

Film camera

Early photography was strictly for the experts. American manufacturer George Eastman changed all that by inventing the Kodak roll film camera. Hot on his heels with an alternative roll film – celluloid photographic film – was Reverend Hannibal Goodwin. Budding photographers simply had to snap their shots then send the camera off to have the film developed. Soon, everyone wanted a camera!

The birth of photography

The first practical photographic process was invented by Niepce's partner Louis Daguerre. He used silvered copper plates to capture the image, producing one-off "positive" photographs that couldn't be copied. But it was Englishman William Fox Talbot who invented the negative-positive process we still use today. This involves taking "negative" images – such that dark areas are light and light areas dark – from which multiple "positive" copies can be made.

1839

Ancient lighthouses

Long ago, people lit bonfires to guide ships at sea. Then somebody had the bright idea of lighting them on top of tall towers so they could be seen from further away. The greatest lighthouse of all time was the Egyptian Pharos of Alexandria. Soaring 134m (440ft) into the sky, it was one of the Seven Wonders of the Ancient World.

It's an ancient wonder!

Fire!

185BC

A middle-of-the-road invention

1934

Five, six, seven cats!

Cat's eyes

While driving home one dark night, British road contractor Percy Shaw was saved from veering off the road by the eyes of a cat gleaming in his headlights. This inspired him to invent "cat's eyes", a device with reflective lenses that could be set in the middle of the road to guide drivers at night.

Fresnel lens

Lenses had long been used in lighthouses to focus the beam of light when Frenchman Augustin Fresnel invented a new kind of lens. Made up of a series of glass rings, Fresnel's lens could be made far bigger than a normal lens and was therefore capable of casting light further out to sea.

Can you see what's at sea?

1286

They're pinching my nose!

You're making a spectacle of yourself

1822

Binoculars

Binoculars are simply two telescopes mounted side by side. Prisms inside bend the light back and forth to give the effect of a long telescope squeezed into a short tube.

I can't see anything

c1880

Spectacles

Venetian glass-makers were possibly the first to make spectacles for improving poor vision. Known as "little disks for the eyes", early models had convex lenses for reading and close-up work and were hinged in the middle for clipping on to the nose.

c840

Camera obscura

The Chinese were the first to project an image of the surrounding landscape through a pinhole and onto the wall of a darkened room. By the 1660s, pinholes had been replaced by lenses and the camera obscura (meaning "darkened room") had shrunk to a more portable size, making it popular with artists.

How obscure

You took your time!

It's brilliant!

I'm camera shy!

1826

The first photograph

All that was needed to turn a camera obscura into a camera was a way of capturing, or fixing, the image. The first person to do so was French scientist Nicéphore Niepce, using light-sensitive tar. The problem was, it took him up to eight hours to take a single photograph!

SEEING IS BELIEVING

Lenses were probably invented in China more than 1,000 years ago. They appeared in Europe in about 1270, where they were originally used in spectacles and magnifying glasses to improve vision. By the 17th century, they were being incorporated into powerful new instruments designed to view objects that were either too far away or too small to see with the naked eye. Telescopes and microscopes heralded a new age in scientific research and transformed the way we see our world and the cosmos beyond.

WANTED

...gulp!

It's him!

Beyond belief

In 1609, Italian astronomer Galileo Galilei became the first person to view the heavens through a telescope. But he soon got into trouble when he claimed his observations showed that the Earth revolved around the Sun, contradicting the Church's belief that the Earth was at the centre of the Universe. He was thrown into jail, under threat of death, until he took it all back!

The lens

Lenses are curved pieces of glass that work by bending, or refracting, light rays passing through them. There are two types of lens: convex and concave, each of which works according to the way it bends light (see opposite). Convex lenses are used to make small objects look bigger; concave lenses make distant objects look closer (but smaller).

The bigger the better!

This is huge!

It's larger than life

c1200

1933

Small is the new big

Electron microscope

Powerful light microscopes can only magnify up to 2,000 times, and, as the magnification goes up, the sharpness of the image goes down. So in 1933 German physicist Ernst Ruska invented a new kind of microscope that used an electron beam instead of light, which gave much better definition. Modern electron microscopes magnify more than a million times to show molecules.

1674

Yup, it's tiny

Can you see it?

Leeuwenhoek's microscope

Dutch draper Antoni van Leeuwenhoek built at

1600

See anything?

Nope... I think we've squashed the ant!

Compound microscope

The compound microscope – that is, a microscope with two or more lenses – was probably invented by Dutch spectacle-maker Hans Janssen in about 1600.

Microscopic enquiry

English scientist Robert Hooke built one of the first successful microscopes. Called a compound microscope, it had a second lens, or eyepiece, to enlarge the magnified image. Hooke used it to study tiny animals and plants, publishing his findings in 1665 in a famous book called *Micrographia*, which featured a huge drawing of a flea 60cm (2ft) long!

Observer views image of specimen through eyepiece

Specially designed lighting system focuses light on specimen

Yum!

Large "eyepiece" lens magnifies the image

Screw fitting raises or lowers microscope to focus it

Small but powerful "objective" lens magnifies the specimen

Specimen

1999

Chandra space telescope
A new kind of telescope was launched into space in 1999. Forming part of NASA's Chandra observatory, it is designed to collect X-rays and is used for studying supernovae, black holes, and dark matter.

So many stars!

Hubble space telescope
In 1990, the Hubble space telescope was launched into orbit to study emissions such as ultra-violet light that don't penetrate the Earth's atmosphere. It can view objects up to 10 billion light years away, seeing much further into space than Earth-based telescopes.

NASA

1990

Great reception

Radio telescope
US radio engineer Grote Reber built a new kind of telescope in his back garden in 1937. Designed to collect radio waves instead of light waves, and therefore show aspects of the Universe not visible to the eye, his radio telescope was the only one of its kind for almost 10 years.

1937

Herschel's telescope
In 1789, British astronomer William Herschel built the largest reflecting telescope of his day. Almost 12m (40ft) long with a 1.2m (4ft) mirror, it was so big it had to be supported on scaffolding and moved around on circular tracks to view different parts of the night sky.

I'm on top of the world!

Up close and personal

Such a starry night!

1663

1608

1789

Refracting telescope
In 1608, Dutch spectacle-maker Hans Lippershey built what is often regarded as the first telescope, based on his discovery that a pair of lenses could make distant objects look closer. He called his invention a "looker" and thought it might be useful in warfare. Galileo built his own telescope (shown here) the following year.

Reflecting telescope
Early refracting or lens-based telescopes gave images with coloured edges. In 1663, Scottish mathematician James Gregory solved this problem by swapping the objective lens for a concave mirror. He'd just invented the reflecting telescope! Five years later, the famous British scientist Isaac Newton designed his own model (shown here) to view the stars.

How lenses work

Image Object

Convex lens
A convex, outward curved lens bends light inwards, making an object look bigger and further away than it actually is.

Object Image

Concave lens
A concave, inward curved lens bends light outwards, making a distant object look smaller and closer than it actually is.

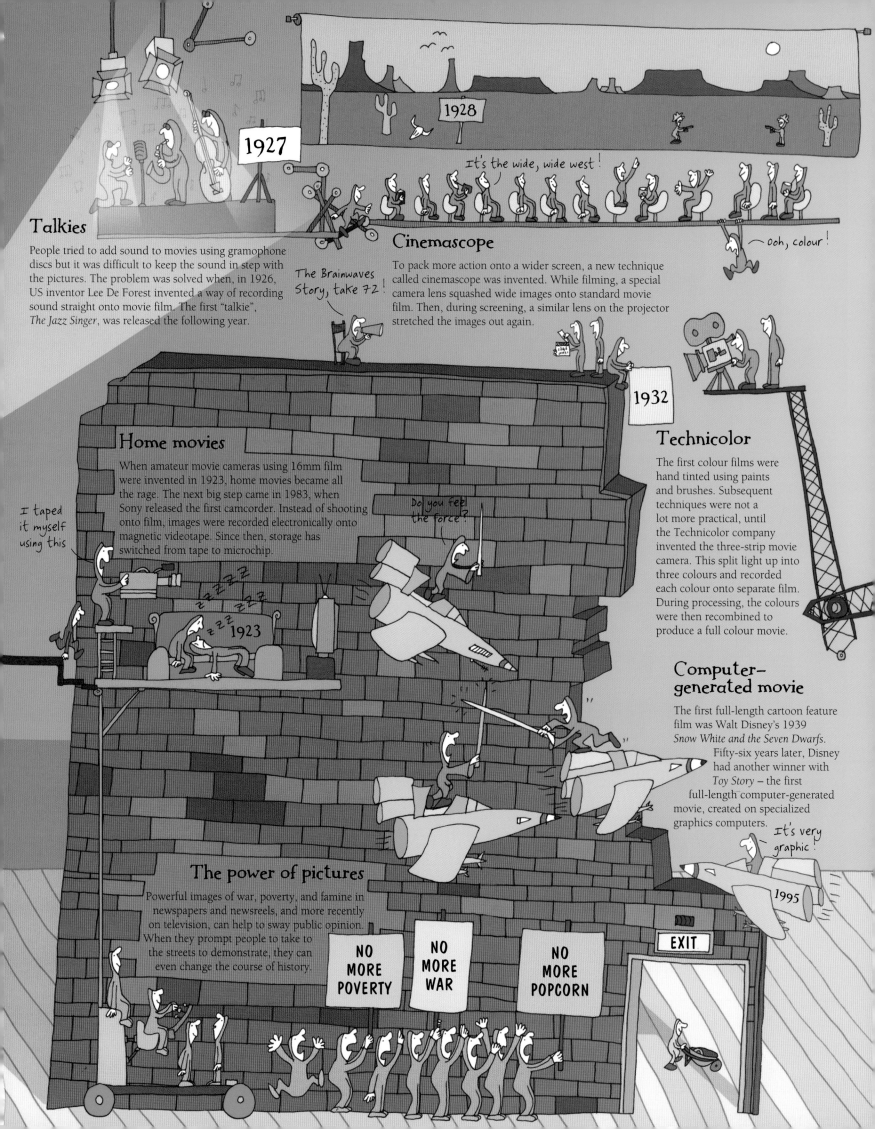

Talkies

People tried to add sound to movies using gramophone discs but it was difficult to keep the sound in step with the pictures. The problem was solved when, in 1926, US inventor Lee De Forest invented a way of recording sound straight onto movie film. The first "talkie", *The Jazz Singer*, was released the following year.

1927

1928

It's the wide, wide west!

Ooh, colour!

Cinemascope

To pack more action onto a wider screen, a new technique called cinemascope was invented. While filming, a special camera lens squashed wide images onto standard movie film. Then, during screening, a similar lens on the projector stretched the images out again.

The Brainwaves Story, take 72!

1932

Technicolor

The first colour films were hand tinted using paints and brushes. Subsequent techniques were not a lot more practical, until the Technicolor company invented the three-strip movie camera. This split light up into three colours and recorded each colour onto separate film. During processing, the colours were then recombined to produce a full colour movie.

Home movies

When amateur movie cameras using 16mm film were invented in 1923, home movies became all the rage. The next big step came in 1983, when Sony released the first camcorder. Instead of shooting onto film, images were recorded electronically onto magnetic videotape. Since then, storage has switched from tape to microchip.

I taped it myself using this

Do you feel the force?

1923

Computer-generated movie

The first full-length cartoon feature film was Walt Disney's 1939 *Snow White and the Seven Dwarfs*. Fifty-six years later, Disney had another winner with *Toy Story* – the first full-length computer-generated movie, created on specialized graphics computers.

It's very graphic!

1995

The power of pictures

Powerful images of war, poverty, and famine in newspapers and newsreels, and more recently on television, can help to sway public opinion. When they prompt people to take to the streets to demonstrate, they can even change the course of history.

NO MORE POVERTY

NO MORE WAR

NO MORE POPCORN

EXIT

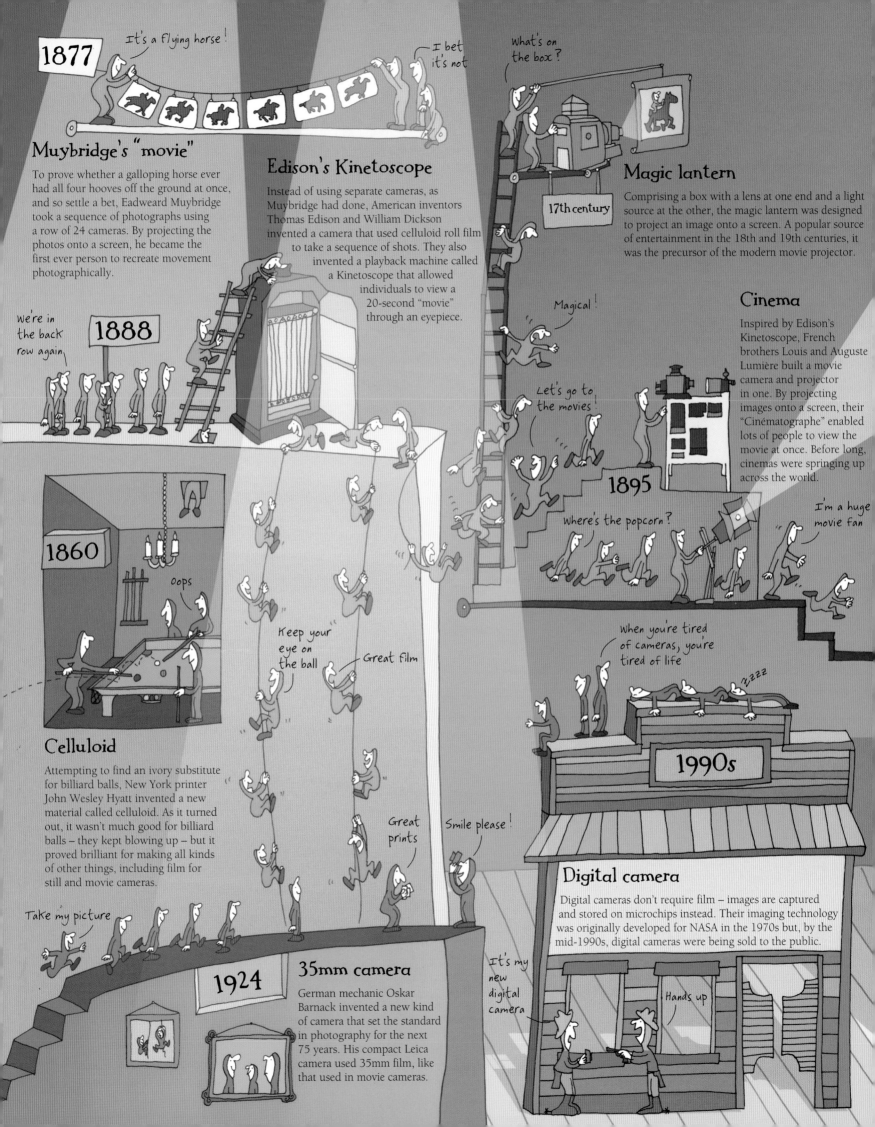

1877

Muybridge's "movie"

To prove whether a galloping horse ever had all four hooves off the ground at once, and so settle a bet, Eadweard Muybridge took a sequence of photographs using a row of 24 cameras. By projecting the photos onto a screen, he became the first ever person to recreate movement photographically.

Edison's Kinetoscope

Instead of using separate cameras, as Muybridge had done, American inventors Thomas Edison and William Dickson invented a camera that used celluloid roll film to take a sequence of shots. They also invented a playback machine called a Kinetoscope that allowed individuals to view a 20-second "movie" through an eyepiece.

Magic lantern

Comprising a box with a lens at one end and a light source at the other, the magic lantern was designed to project an image onto a screen. A popular source of entertainment in the 18th and 19th centuries, it was the precursor of the modern movie projector.

17th century

Cinema

Inspired by Edison's Kinetoscope, French brothers Louis and Auguste Lumière built a movie camera and projector in one. By projecting images onto a screen, their "Cinématographe" enabled lots of people to view the movie at once. Before long, cinemas were springing up across the world.

1895

1888

1860

Celluloid

Attempting to find an ivory substitute for billiard balls, New York printer John Wesley Hyatt invented a new material called celluloid. As it turned out, it wasn't much good for billiard balls – they kept blowing up – but it proved brilliant for making all kinds of other things, including film for still and movie cameras.

1990s

Digital camera

Digital cameras don't require film – images are captured and stored on microchips instead. Their imaging technology was originally developed for NASA in the 1970s but, by the mid-1990s, digital cameras were being sold to the public.

1924

35mm camera

German mechanic Oskar Barnack invented a new kind of camera that set the standard in photography for the next 75 years. His compact Leica camera used 35mm film, like that used in movie cameras.

Richard Arkwright

Factories didn't exist when British barber Richard Arkwright invented his water-powered spinning frame. He went on to mechanize every stage of manufacture, gathering all his workers together in huge factories. Soon, other people were building factories too, and Arkwright became known as the "Father of the Factory System".

1732–1792

1765–1825

Eli Whitney

American industrialist Eli Whitney is famous for inventing a device called the cotton gin, used for separating cotton fibre from the seeds. He went on to invent a way of mass-producing guns for the US Army by making thousands of identical parts that were interchangeable. This method became known as the American system of manufacture.

1791–1867

Michael Faraday

The son of a blacksmith, English scientist Michael Faraday became known as the "Father of Electricity". Having demonstrated the principle of the electric motor and generator, he left it up to others to develop his ideas and build practical models.

Please, no more steps

1706–1790

eed hand?

Benjamin Franklin

One of America's greatest citizens, Benjamin Franklin did a lot more than invent the lightning conductor. He was also a writer, printer, and statesman, who helped to gain his country's independence from Britain and establish the United States of America.

Stop!

Yippee!

Well he kept himself busy

1833–1896

This man had principles!

Great beard

1452–1519

Leonardo da Vinci

Italian painter, sculptor, and engineer Leonardo da Vinci was an amazing man. He filled his notebooks with thousands of drawings of his inventions and discoveries, from war engines to flying machines. The only problem was, most of them were never built!

Alfred Nobel

The Swedish inventor of dynamite, Alfred Nobel, amassed a fortune manufacturing explosives. Upon his death, he bequeathed much of his money to a series of annual prizes, for science, literature, and peace, that still bears his name. He even has a synthetic element named after him – nobelium.

c287–212BC

Archimedes

Greek mathematician Archimedes is most famous for shouting "Eureka!" as he jumped out of the bath, and giving his name to a pump that he didn't actually invent! But he did invent other things, such as siege engines and formulas for working out the area and circumference of a circle.

Who invented exhibitions?

ook! An exhibition of amous thingummybobs

Famous Inventors

Inventors come from all walks of life, from artists and barbers to scientists and statesmen. Some, such as Archimedes and Thomas Jefferson, are better known for other achievements in their lives. People like Richard Arkwright and Thomas Edison, on the other hand, are famous for inventing things that have changed the way we live. What they all share in common is a passion for exploring ideas, solving problems, and never giving up until the job is done.

Mattie Knight

American "Queen of the Paper Bags", Mattie Knight made her name inventing a machine for manufacturing square-bottomed paper bags for carrying groceries. She developed her first invention aged 12, creating a safety device for textile machinery.

1838–1914

Josephine Cochran

Tired of the servants breaking her best china, rich socialite Josephine Cochran declared, "If nobody else is going to invent a dishwashing machine, I'll do it myself!" And so she did, even setting up her own company to manufacture them.

1841–1913

Thomas Edison

Despite the fact his teacher called him "addled", Thomas Edison grew up to become the world's most prolific inventor, with 1,097 patents to his name. Working up to 20 hours a day in his "invention factory", supported by a team of up to 3,600 staff, he devised everything from movie cameras and projectors to electric pens and light bulbs.

1847–1931

1847–1922

She looks washed out

It could catch on

Guglielmo Marconi

Italian inventor Guglielmo Marconi gave the first public demonstration of his wireless telegraphy in London, having had his original apparatus torn apart by suspicious customs officials. Soon, wireless telegraphy was spreading across the world.

1874–1937

Alexander Graham Bell

Like his father before him, Alexander Graham Bell taught deaf people how to speak. He was also a keen inventor, and it was while developing a harmonic telegraph, which sent messages as musical notes, that he had the bright idea of transmitting speech instead. So it was that he invented the telephone.

Frank Whittle

When RAF pilot Frank Whittle patented his design for a jet engine in 1930, he couldn't get the British Air Ministry interested. They finally decided to back him in 1939, but by then it was too late for his invention to influence the course of World War II.

1907–1996

We're rich!

I need a new job

Steve Wozniak and Steve Jobs

In order to dispel fears that their personal computer was complicated, electronics hobbyists Steve Wozniak and Steve Jobs gave their new company the simplest name they could think of – Apple! Within a decade, they were selling 10 million Apple computers a year in the USA alone.

Born 1950 and 1955 respectively

So many clever people

I feel inspired

Born 1923

Stephanie Kwolek

American research scientist Stephanie Kwolek is best known for inventing a synthetic fibre, called Kevlar, that is five times stronger than steel. Patented in 1966, Kevlar is used to make a host of items, including bulletproof vests, safety helmets, and trampolines.

Postcards!

That was great!

Industrial Revolution

Once water and steam power came on the scene, it no longer made sense for spinners and weavers to work at home as they had done previously. Instead, they crowded together into noisy, grimy factories in newly built towns, where the hours were long and the pay poor. Steam had helped to power an Industrial Revolution and people's lives were changed for ever!

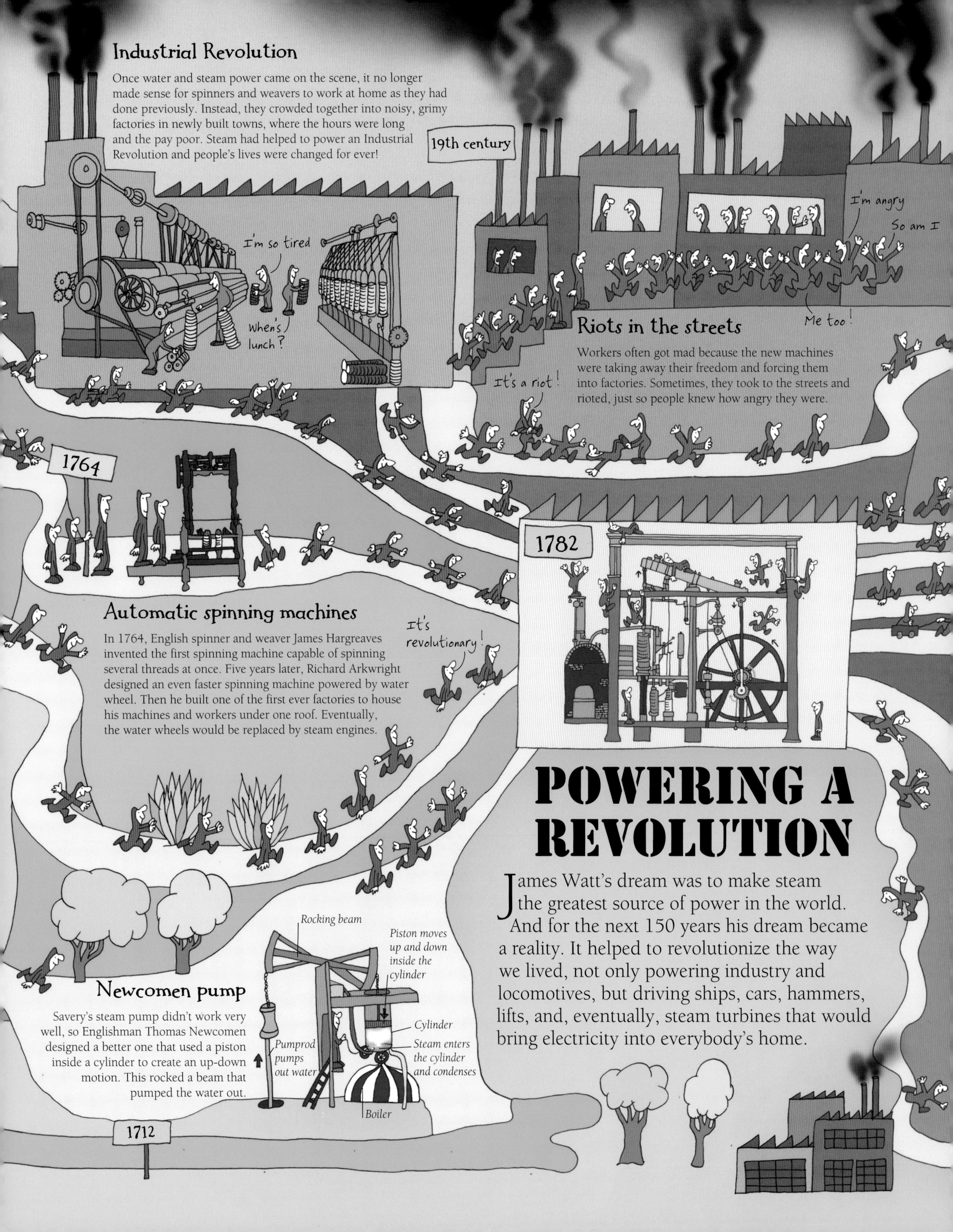

19th century

I'm so tired

When's lunch?

I'm angry

So am I

Me too!

Riots in the streets

Workers often got mad because the new machines were taking away their freedom and forcing them into factories. Sometimes, they took to the streets and rioted, just so people knew how angry they were.

It's a riot!

1764

Automatic spinning machines

In 1764, English spinner and weaver James Hargreaves invented the first spinning machine capable of spinning several threads at once. Five years later, Richard Arkwright designed an even faster spinning machine powered by water wheel. Then he built one of the first ever factories to house his machines and workers under one roof. Eventually, the water wheels would be replaced by steam engines.

It's revolutionary!

1782

POWERING A REVOLUTION

James Watt's dream was to make steam the greatest source of power in the world. And for the next 150 years his dream became a reality. It helped to revolutionize the way we lived, not only powering industry and locomotives, but driving ships, cars, hammers, lifts, and, eventually, steam turbines that would bring electricity into everybody's home.

Rocking beam

Piston moves up and down inside the cylinder

Newcomen pump

Savery's steam pump didn't work very well, so Englishman Thomas Newcomen designed a better one that used a piston inside a cylinder to create an up-down motion. This rocked a beam that pumped the water out.

Pumprod pumps out water

Cylinder

Steam enters the cylinder and condenses

Boiler

1712

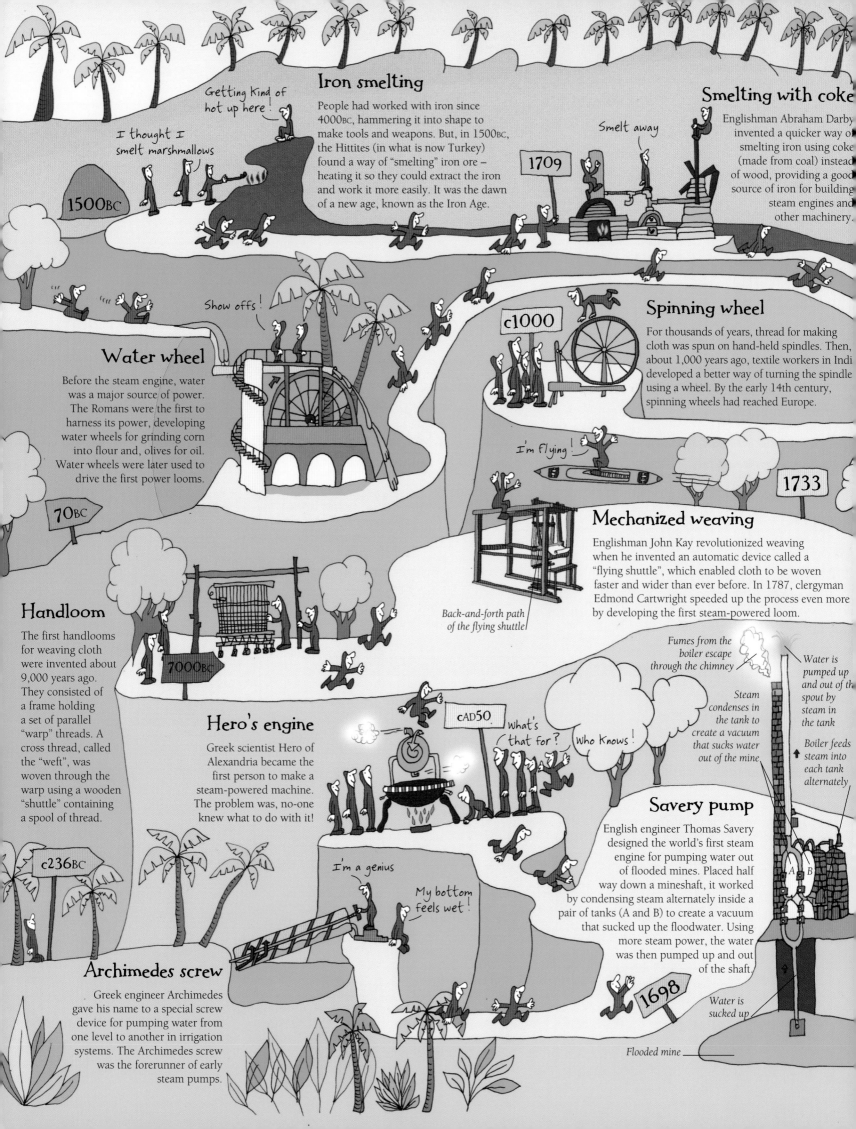

Iron smelting

People had worked with iron since 4000BC, hammering it into shape to make tools and weapons. But, in 1500BC, the Hittites (in what is now Turkey) found a way of "smelting" iron ore – heating it so they could extract the iron and work it more easily. It was the dawn of a new age, known as the Iron Age.

Getting kind of hot up here!

I thought I smelt marshmallows

1500BC

Smelting with coke

Englishman Abraham Darby invented a quicker way of smelting iron using coke (made from coal) instead of wood, providing a good source of iron for building steam engines and other machinery.

Smelt away

1709

Water wheel

Before the steam engine, water was a major source of power. The Romans were the first to harness its power, developing water wheels for grinding corn into flour and, olives for oil. Water wheels were later used to drive the first power looms.

Show offs!

70BC

Spinning wheel

For thousands of years, thread for making cloth was spun on hand-held spindles. Then, about 1,000 years ago, textile workers in India developed a better way of turning the spindle using a wheel. By the early 14th century, spinning wheels had reached Europe.

c1000

I'm flying!

1733

Mechanized weaving

Englishman John Kay revolutionized weaving when he invented an automatic device called a "flying shuttle", which enabled cloth to be woven faster and wider than ever before. In 1787, clergyman Edmond Cartwright speeded up the process even more by developing the first steam-powered loom.

Back-and-forth path of the flying shuttle

Handloom

The first handlooms for weaving cloth were invented about 9,000 years ago. They consisted of a frame holding a set of parallel "warp" threads. A cross thread, called the "weft", was woven through the warp using a wooden "shuttle" containing a spool of thread.

7000BC

Hero's engine

Greek scientist Hero of Alexandria became the first person to make a steam-powered machine. The problem was, no-one knew what to do with it!

cAD50

What's that for?

Who knows!

Archimedes screw

Greek engineer Archimedes gave his name to a special screw device for pumping water from one level to another in irrigation systems. The Archimedes screw was the forerunner of early steam pumps.

c236BC

I'm a genius

My bottom feels wet!

Savery pump

English engineer Thomas Savery designed the world's first steam engine for pumping water out of flooded mines. Placed half way down a mineshaft, it worked by condensing steam alternately inside a pair of tanks (A and B) to create a vacuum that sucked up the floodwater. Using more steam power, the water was then pumped up and out of the shaft.

1698

Fumes from the boiler escape through the chimney

Water is pumped up and out of the spout by steam in the tank

Steam condenses in the tank to create a vacuum that sucks water out of the mine

Boiler feeds steam into each tank alternately

Water is sucked up

Flooded mine

STEAM MACHINE

James Watt

Until the 18th century, the main sources of power were water, wind, and horses. The development of the steam engine changed all that, and life was never the same again. The first steam engines were used to pump water out of mines, but in 1782 Scottish engineer James Watt built a new engine that was soon put to work driving machinery. Then Richard Trevithick had the brilliant idea of using steam power to pull carriages along rails and the rest, as they say, is history!

Watt a guy

King of steam

When Scottish engineer James Watt was asked to mend an old steam engine, he realized he could do far better and by 1769 had designed a much more efficient model. With his partner Matthew Boulton, he went on to manufacture steam engines that sold across the world.

The rotary steam engine

In common with other early steam engines, Watt's first model could only create an up-down motion, ideal for pumping water. Then, in 1782, he designed a new engine that converted the up-down action into a circular, or rotary, motion using special gears called sun and planet gears. This meant his engines could be used instead of water wheels to drive textile mills and other machinery.

3. Beam is rocked up and down by the moving piston

4. Governor regulates the engine's speed

5. Sun and planet gears, turned by the rocking beam, translate the up-down motion into a rotary motion

2. Steam fed into the cylinder, forcing the piston inside the cylinder up and down

6. Flywheel helps to keep the engine running smoothly

1. Boiler turns water into steam

Stephenson's Rocket

1829

In 1829, a contest was held to find the best locomotive ever. Stephenson's *Rocket* won with flying colours and was soon put to work on the Manchester and Liverpool line, the first regular passenger service.

Death on the tracks

1830

Stephenson's *Rocket* was the fastest locomotive of its day, with a top speed of 56kph (35mph). Many people feared that they'd suffocate or go mad travelling at such high speeds. But it wasn't suffocation that killed poor William Huskisson – he was run over by the *Rocket* on its first day in service!

Aaargh, I've met my death!

Crossing continents

1869

The first railway to straddle an entire continent was built across the USA during the 1860s. Starting out from both east and west, and crossing over 3,000km (1,860 miles) of wilderness, the two lines finally came together at Promontory Point, Utah, in May 1869. A nation was united and a journey that used to last six months now took seven days!

Where's it gone?

Mind the gap!

Steam locomotive

1803

In 1803, English engineer Richard Trevithick built the world's first steam locomotive, for hauling coal. He took his idea to London in 1808, where he built a circular track for his new engine – called *Catch Me Who Can* – offering delighted passengers a ride for a shilling a go.

All aboard

1863

Public railway

825

The first public railway was only 20km (13 miles) long. Set up in 1825, it carried goods and passengers between Stockton and Darlington in the north of England, powered by engineer Robert Stephenson's *Locomotion No. 1*.

Going underground

In 1863 the world's first underground service, powered by steam train, was launched in London. On the opening day, even future Prime Minister William Gladstone came along for the ride!

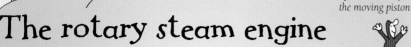

Steam locomotive

[In] the early days of railway, George Stephenson's *Rocket* became the model for [fu]ture locomotive design. At its heart lay a boiler containing about 150 fire tubes. [H]ot gases from the firebox passed through the tubes to boil the water and create [st]eam. The steam drove a piston back and forth inside a "double-action" cylinder [(se]e right), which made the wheels go round.

4. Hot gases collect in the smokebox and escape through the smokestack

Water inside the boiler

3. Steam passes down the steam pipe to the cylinders

2. Hot gases pass along the fire tubes, causing the water to boil

1. Coal burns in the firebox, creating heat

Smokestack

Firebox

[S]team passes into the cylinder and [d]rives the piston back and forth

Front wheels help carry weight and guide the engine

6. Piston rod drives the wheels round, via the driving rod

Driving rod turns the wheels

Large wheels drive the locomotive forward

How a double-action cylinder works

In a double-action cylinder, high-pressure steam enters the cylinder first on one side, then on the other, forcing the piston back and forth with each stroke. This double action helps to make the engine more efficient. The motion is then carried to the wheels via the piston rod. The piston rod also pushes the slide valve back and forth, controlling the flow of steam into the cylinder.

Steam in

1. *Steam enters the cylinder via the left inlet valve*

Slide valve blocks the right inlet valve

Valve rod

Cylinder

2. *Piston is driven right by the steam*

3. *Piston rod transfers the motion to the wheels, via the driving rod*

4. *Slide valve is driven left by the piston rod, to block the left inlet valve*

7. *Exhaust steam exits via the exhaust valve*

5. *Steam now enters the cylinder through the right inlet valve*

6. *Piston is driven left by the steam, pulling the slide valve back again and driving the wheels through a full revolution*

1879

Electric locomotive

The first practical electric train was built in 1879 by German [e]ngineer Werner von Siemens for an exhibition in Berlin. Faster, quieter, and easier to run than steam trains, electric trains soon started to replace their old rivals.

1941

Big Boy

The biggest ever steam locomotive was the USA's mighty *Big Boy*, built in 1941. Used for hauling freight across mountains, it weighed a staggering 600 tonnes (590 tons) – almost as much as 100 elephants!

1964

Bullet train

Introduced in 1964, the Japanese *Shinkansen*, or "bullet train", was the first of a new breed of high-speed electric trains, travelling up to 210kph (130mph).

2003

Diesel locomotive

First developed in Germany in 1912, diesel trains such as the American high-speed *Zephyr* became very successful in the 1930s. Along with electric trains, they led to the demise of the steam train.

1912

Built for speed

In 1938, the British locomotive *Mallard* reached a maximum speed of 205kph (127mph), making it the fastest ever steam locomotive – a record that still stands today.

1938

Maglev trains

The world's first magnetic levitation (maglev) railway opened in Shanghai, China, in 2003. In a maglev system, the train literally floats above a single track, propelled forward by magnetic fields in the line. Reaching speeds of up to 430kph (270mph), maglev trains may represent the railways of the future.

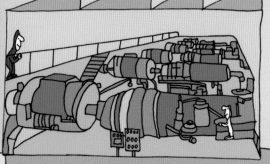

1888

Power to the people

Before long, Parson's steam turbines were set to work in large power plants generating electricity for people's homes. As well as providing heat and light, electricity was soon used to power a vast range of new labour-saving devices, from kettles and toasters to vacuum cleaners and washing machines.

Power to us

Power to me

Power to my toaster!

1853

Safety lift

A fear of accidents made early steam-powered lifts unpopular. Then American mechanic Elisha Otis invented a safety mechanism which he demonstrated by standing in a lift while an axe-man cut the cable. The locking system worked and Otis lived to tell the tale! Within four years the first safety passenger lift had been installed in a shop in New York.

It works

Fantastic view!

...ship

...g, before the Wright ...ers took to the skies ...e first aeroplane, French ...tor Henri Giffard built ...am-powered airship that ...ew over Paris, covering ...m (20 miles).

...team turbine ship

...ing invented the steam turbine, ...es Parsons went on to build the ...t steam-turbine powered ship – ...the *Turbinia*. Before long, steam ...es were powering the awesome ...readnought battleships and the ...gant luxury liners that ruled the ...waves in the early 20th century.

1894

Skyscraper

Until the late 19th century, buildings were rarely built higher than six storeys – a reasonable height for people to climb on foot. But with the invention of the safety lift, combined with new building techniques, buildings grew taller and taller, giving rise to the skyscraper. The first skyscraper was the 10-storey Home Insurance Building in Chicago, USA, built by architect William Le Baron Jenney.

I'm sky-high

1885

A great age to be in

Age of luxury liners

Steam cars

By 1900, road vehicles powered by steam engines had been around for more than 100 years. But with the advent of the petrol-driven internal combustion engine, the race was on to see whether steam or petrol power would win the day. In 1906, it looked like steam was in the lead, when the American Stanley Steamer reached a record 200kph (127mph).

1906

Full steam ahead!

I want one of those!

1860s

Steam turbine

For more than 100 years steam engines were based on Watt's design. Then Irish engineer Charles Parsons invented the quieter steam turbine, which turned a series of fan-like blades mounted on a central shaft. Its effect was so great that Parsons became known as "the man who invented the 20th century".

Steam turbine generator

It spins!

1884

Someones invented the 20th century

What a good idea!

This stinks

Hooray, the river's clean

Death and disease

The new factory towns were cheaply built and horribly overcrowded, with families of six or more often crammed together in a single room. The air was thick with factory fumes and, without proper lavatories and clean drinking water, streets and rivers teemed with filth. Diseases such as cholera were widespread and many people died young.

Cleaning up the act

In London in the 1860s, engineer Joseph Bazalgette built the first modern sewage system, using huge steam engines to pump human waste into the river, far away from the city. At last people had clean drinking water, and cholera became a thing of the past.

1852

Don't get carried away!

1839

Steam pressure in the cylinder lifts the hammer up

Crane for lifting the iron block

Hammer drops as steam is released from the cylinder

Iron block shaped by the falling hammer

Steam hammer

Englishman James Nasmyth put steam to good use when he built the first successful steam hammer. It was designed to forge the enormous iron parts used in industry and shipping, such as in the building of Brunel's mighty *Great Britain*.

Steamship

Frenchman Marquis de Jouffroy d'Abbans built the first practical steamboat in 1783. But it was 36 years before a steamship made the first trans-Atlantic crossing – in 1819, the US paddle steamer *Savannah* crossed in 27 days.

1783

I can see the sea!

That's blown it

1843

1859

Screw propulsion

Paddle steamers weren't very efficient, so English engineer Isambard Kingdom Brunel set out to improve their design. The result was the *Great Britain* – the first ocean-going steamship to be built of iron and driven by screw propeller instead of paddle.

Disaster at sea

Brunel's next ship, the *Great Eastern*, was gigantic – almost six times bigger than any other ship built to date! But on a trial run in 1859 a steam pipe burst, causing one of the funnels to explode and killing six people. It was all too much for Brunel, who died a few days later.

1769

Watch out!

Oh, a wall!

Cugnot steam carriage

Frenchman Nicolas Cugnot became the first person to build a road vehicle powered by steam engine. But his design wasn't very successful and, on his first day out, he lost control and crashed it into a wall!

FANTASTIC INVENTIONS

Over the last 150 years, the desire to save lives, improve transport, or simply make everyday living that little bit easier has given rise to some of the world's strangest inventions. Many, such as the eagle-powered flying machine, were so silly that it's difficult to believe anyone ever thought they stood a chance of success. Others, like the horse-shaped steam tram, actually became a reality. And then there were the ones that were never supposed to work in the first place!

ENTRANCE

Walking on water

An unfortunate incident at sea may have prompted American inventor Henry Rowlands to invent this precarious "apparatus for walking on water". It comprised two tiny boats joined together by swivelling bars. The user stood on the decks and propelled the boats forward with his feet, steadying himself with the upright poles.

1858

I have a sinking feeling about this!

1865

Eagle power

The 19th century witnessed numerous attempts to build a flying machine, but few resulted in such a bizarre contraption as this one. The aim was to harness the power of nature by using a ring of eagles to carry a man aloft in a metal cage.

This way

I feel sleepy just watching

Rocking machine

One enterprising inventor decided that a rocking chair could be put to better use than simply soothing the nerves. So he rigged up a chair with a series of levers, pulleys, and ropes so that the user could rock the baby and churn butter at the same time!

1873

Is it a think tank?

I'll be taking off any time now!

Those fish look hungry!

1877

Water suit

Designing life preservers was an obsession with Victorian inventors. American Traugott Beek devised this ingenious suit made of sailcloth attached to circular metal tubes. Containing enough food and water for a month, it enabled anyone unlucky enough to be shipwrecked to survive for weeks in the water.

Ayres's aerial machine

The renowned journal *Scientific American* had high hopes for Dr Ayres's new flying machine. Powered by compressed air and a frantically pedalling pilot, in theory the craft would be lifted into the air by a series of horizontal propellers. In practice, it would have made a better bedstead than an aeroplane!

1885

Steam horse

When steam trams first appeared in San Francisco they caused havoc on the streets, scaring all the horses. So one Mr Matheson designed a tram shaped like a horse. With a steam engine in its rump, and running on gas to avoid belching smoke, it seemed to solve the problem.

Giddyup

1876

I see cakes!

CAFÉ

Suitcase lifejacket

What better way to ensure safety at sea than to have a suitcase that doubles as a lifejacket? A German named Krankel did just that by inventing a case with two removable panels. The user simply took these out, sealed the hole with a rubber ring and slipped the case over his body.

1880s

I want one

Uniwheel

Even after the invention of the bicycle, some people still thought the future lay with single-wheeled cycles, or uniwheels. Designs such as this one were almost impossible to steer and, with spokes on either side, seemingly impossible to get into!

1884

How does he get out?

well he's in!

Self-raising hat

What was a Victorian gentleman to do upon encountering a lady if he had his hands full? The answer lay in James Boyle's self-tipping hat. By simply nodding, the wearer activated a clockwork mechanism that automatically tipped his hat for him!

I take off my hat to him!

1896

Bicycle shower

One enterprising cyclist had the bright idea of combining the morning shower with a bit of exercise. His "Vélodouche" used pedal power to pump water into the shower. The harder you pedalled, the more powerful the shower!

1896

Umbrellas for sale!

Shhhhh!....

1971

Patting the baby

American inventor Thomas Zelenka, possibly tired of patting the baby to sleep, invented an electrically powered mechanical arm to do it for him. Attached to the side of the cot, the arm pats a baby's bottom to send the tiny tot off to sleep.

It's on a roll

1976

Rolling ball

Designed by Alessandro Dandini, this curious marine craft comprises a large motorized ball with two cabins attached on either side. In theory, if something goes wrong, the cabins can be released by firing explosive bolts. The problem is, having released one cabin, the whole contraption would become unbalanced and keel over on its side!

Crazy

Bizarre

Nope, just weird

Chindogo

Japanese comedian Kenji Kawakami created a craze for nonsensical devices when he started inventing Chindogo – meaning "weird tool". Designed to create more problems than they solve, they include a solar-powered torch, a portable zebra crossing, and a motorized noodle fork.

1990s

Is it safe to cross?

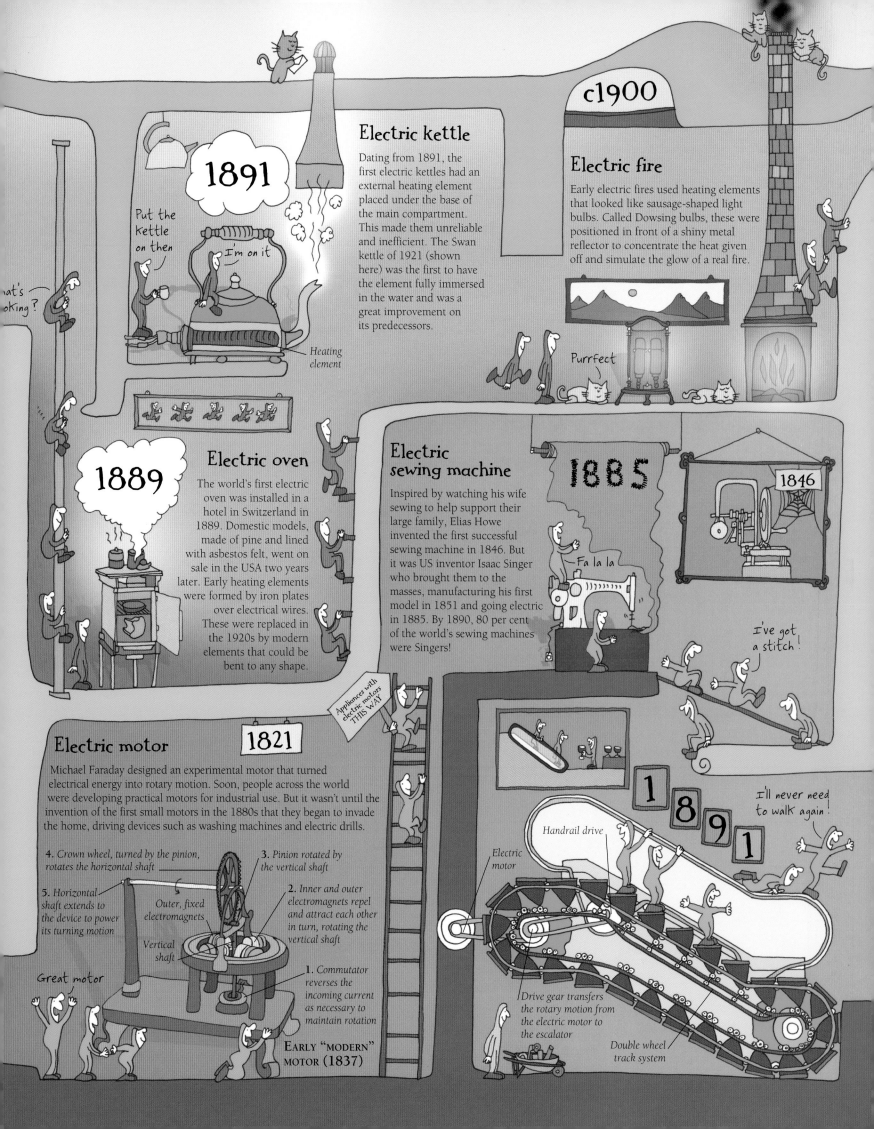

Electric kettle

1891

Dating from 1891, the first electric kettles had an external heating element placed under the base of the main compartment. This made them unreliable and inefficient. The Swan kettle of 1921 (shown here) was the first to have the element fully immersed in the water and was a great improvement on its predecessors.

Put the kettle on then

I'm on it

What's cooking?

Heating element

c1900

Electric fire

Early electric fires used heating elements that looked like sausage-shaped light bulbs. Called Dowsing bulbs, these were positioned in front of a shiny metal reflector to concentrate the heat given off and simulate the glow of a real fire.

Purrfect

Electric oven

1889

The world's first electric oven was installed in a hotel in Switzerland in 1889. Domestic models, made of pine and lined with asbestos felt, went on sale in the USA two years later. Early heating elements were formed by iron plates over electrical wires. These were replaced in the 1920s by modern elements that could be bent to any shape.

Electric sewing machine

1885

Inspired by watching his wife sewing to help support their large family, Elias Howe invented the first successful sewing machine in 1846. But it was US inventor Isaac Singer who brought them to the masses, manufacturing his first model in 1851 and going electric in 1885. By 1890, 80 per cent of the world's sewing machines were Singers!

Fa la la

1846

I've got a stitch!

Appliances with electric motors THIS WAY

Electric motor

1821

Michael Faraday designed an experimental motor that turned electrical energy into rotary motion. Soon, people across the world were developing practical motors for industrial use. But it wasn't until the invention of the first small motors in the 1880s that they began to invade the home, driving devices such as washing machines and electric drills.

4. Crown wheel, turned by the pinion, rotates the horizontal shaft

3. Pinion rotated by the vertical shaft

5. Horizontal shaft extends to the device to power its turning motion

Outer, fixed electromagnets

2. Inner and outer electromagnets repel and attract each other in turn, rotating the vertical shaft

Vertical shaft

1. Commutator reverses the incoming current as necessary to maintain rotation

Great motor

EARLY "MODERN" MOTOR (1837)

1891

I'll never need to walk again!

Handrail drive

Electric motor

Drive gear transfers the rotary motion from the electric motor to the escalator

Double wheel track system

Electric toys

18th century

Performing tricks with electricity was once a popular pastime. The electricity generated by this electrical "toy" passed down a sword into a spoonful of alcohol, causing the alcohol to burst into flames, and delighting onlookers.

Lightning conductor

1752

American statesman and scientist Benjamin Franklin risked his life to prove lightning was a form of electricity. He flew a kite in a storm and watched as the lightning passed down the line and sent sparks flying off a metal key tied to the end. Based on his studies, he went on to invent the lightning conductor.

Electric iron

Designed in 1882 by New Yorker Henry Seely, the first electric irons spluttered and hissed, and burnt tiny holes in clothes. The following year, Seely invented a safety iron that was heated on a separate stand. Irons with flexible cords that plugged into light sockets followed in 1891.

1882

Power to the people

Bringing electricity into people's homes didn't just result in a new form of lighting, it caused a domestic revolution. Within a few years, a host of new labour-saving appliances had invaded the home, driven by electric motors or heated by electric elements. They transformed everyday tasks such as washing, cleaning, and cooking, and, as demand for electricity soared, so new ways of making it were sought.

Electric chair

One of the 19th century's more gruesome inventions was the electric chair, developed by Edison's former assistant Harold Brown. In a possible attempt to discredit a rival system, he powered the chair using Westinghouse's alternating current, rather than Edison's direct current. As a result, electrocution became known as "Westinghousing".

1888

1882

Let there be light

City streets were dark and dangerous places at night until gas lamps wer[e] introduced in the early 19th century. Lighting homes was not so simpl[e]. Wax candles were expensive, oil lamps were smelly, and gas lighting gave [off] fumes, stained furniture, and killed the pot plants! In the 1870s, two men independently set out to invent an alternative that was cheap, clean, and c[ould] be controlled by the flick of a switch – the result was the electric light bulb[.]

Edison   Swan

Bright sparks

Although Swan beat Edison to invent the light bulb by a few months, the two men were soon caught up in a legal battle over patent rights. But by 1883 they had seen the light and combined forces to produce the "Ediswan" light bulb!

How light bulbs work

Edison and Swan's light bulbs worked on the principle of "incandescence" – meaning, a filament will glow with heat when an electric current is passed through it. Modern incandescent bulbs work in a similar way, only now they have a tungsten filament instead of carbon, which lasts longer and gives a brighter light.

Glass bulb contains inert gas that prevents the filament burning

Tungsten filament glows when the current passes through it

Glass mount supports the filament

Support wires carry the electric current to the tungsten filament

Screw thread contact to mains electricity

Blazing!

The light bulb

In 1879, British chemist Joseph Swan and US inventor Thomas Edison both demonstrated a practical light bulb, comprising a glowing filament inside a vacuum. The problem had been finding a filament that wouldn't burn away within minutes. After 1,200 experiments using different materials, including fishing line and coconut h[air], Edison discovered that carbonized sewing thread worked best!

Look, it glows without a flame!

Glass bulb

Vacuum inside bulb

Filament made from carbonized thread

And lights without a match!

EDISON'S FIRST ELECTRIC LAMP

1792

1800

1807

It's a pile-up

1831

1866

I wish some[one] would invent [...]

Gas lighting

William Murdock became the first person to install gas lighting, doing so in his home in Cornwall, England, in 1792. By the early 19th century, city streets across Europe and the USA were being lit by gas.

Volta's pile

The first electric battery was invented by Italian scientist Alessandro Volta. Comprising a stack of metal and brine-soaked cardboard disks, Volta's "pile" produced the first reliable current, making experiments into electricity easier to perform.

Arc lights

English chemist Sir Humphrey Davy used a battery to power his invention – the arc light. But arc lights weren't used for street lighting until the 1870s, once a practical power source had been developed. Even then, they were too bright for use in the home.

Electric generator

The course of history was changed in 1831 when English scientist Michael Faraday discovered that by moving a magnet inside a coil of wire he could create, or "induce", an electric current. He had just invented the electric generator.

Leclanché batter[y]

Using a glass jar conta[ining] carbon rods in chemic[als,] French engineer Geor[ges ...] invented a new kind [...] It was the forerunne[r ...] cell batteries, which a[re ...] countless items from [...]

The generator

What good was an electric light bulb without the means of supplying electricity to people's homes? It was Edison who made it feasible, designing an entire electricity supply system, from high-voltage generators and insulated cables to screw sockets and light switches. In 1882, he opened the first public power station in Pearl Street, New York, using generators driven by steam engines to light 13,000 lamps in homes and offices across several city blocks.

EDISON'S PEARL STREET GENERATORS

Flywheel, driven by a steam engine, turns the armature

1. Electromagnet creates a magnetic field

2. Rotating "armature" (wire coil) induces an alternating current (which fluctuates back and forth)

3. "Commutator" turns the alternating current into a direct current

4. Carbon brushes pick up the direct current

5. Electric current flows to homes and offices

Magnetic field created between the magnet's poles

South pole

North pole

Commutator

Wire coil (armature) rotates

Current flows through the circuit

Bulb glows when the current flows through the circuit

Generators at work

Generators work on the principle of "electromagnetic induction" – that is, an electric current can be induced to flow by moving a wire coil inside a magnetic field. In this diagram, the movement is created by turning a handle; Edison used steam engines to do the same job. As generators produce an alternating current (one that fluctuates backwards and forwards), Edison used a device called a commutator to turn it into a direct current (one that flows in one direction only) for sending to homes and offices.

Wonder what's showing tonight?

I love these things but they disturb my sleep

I need sunglasses it's so bright in here

Wow! Is this a light house?

Chaos

That bulb's got no filament

And it's making me green

1880   1882   1888   1901   1912

Bulbs for sale

Within a year of inventing his incandescent bulb, Thomas Edison was selling light bulbs commercially. His new, improved design used carbonized bamboo as a filament and worked for more than 1,100 hours!

Power to Pearl Street

Edison's Pearl Street power station of 1882 kicked off the age of electricity, and soon other power stations using rival systems were opening up across the western world. Edison's biggest rival was George Westinghouse, who supplied alternating current.

Steam turbine power

Irishman Charles Parsons invented a new kind of steam engine – the steam turbine. By 1888 it had been put to work driving electricity generators, and is still used today in modern power stations and large ships such as ocean cruisers.

Fluorescent lighting

In 1901, US electrical engineer Peter Cooper-Hewitt designed a light bulb that worked without a filament. Called a mercury vapour lamp, it had to be tilted to get it going! It wasn't very successful but the idea re-emerged in 1935 as the tubular fluorescent lamp.

Neon signs

French physicist Georges Claude discovered that passing a current through a glass tube filled with neon gas produced a bright red glow. By 1912, he had put his find to practical use and invented the neon sign.

Microwave oven 1946

While doing research into radar, US engineer Percy Spencer realized that microwave emissions had melted a peanut bar in his pocket! After experimenting with eggs and popcorn, he confirmed that microwaves could indeed cook food, and went on to develop the microwave oven.

Now that's fast food

1969 Solar energy

Heat from the sun can also be used to provide electricity. The first solar power station was at Odeillo in France, built to provide energy for scientific experiments. Since then, solar energy has been harnessed for domestic purposes but, for obvious reasons, it works best in sunny countries.

Don't forget your sun cream!

Just recharging my batteries

1927 Jukebox

Built in 1890, the very first jukebox had individual listening tubes and only played one tune! The jukebox as we know it today – an all-electric, amplified, multi-selection player – was introduced by the Automatic Musical Instrument Company in 1927. By 1939, there were more than 350,000 jukeboxes across America.

Shake! *Rattle and roll!*

Nuclear power station

Electricity generators driven by coal- and oil-fired steam turbines powered the age of electricity. Then, in 1954, the Russians built the first nuclear power station in Obninsk, near Moscow, which harnessed the energy of nuclear fission (splitting atoms). Two years later, Calder Hall in England became the world's first large-scale commercial nuclear power station. The big problem with nuclear power though is that its waste product gives off harmful emissions for up to 250,000 years!

1954

Electric razor

Lieutenant Colonel Jacob Schick of the US Army wanted to find a way of shaving without soap and water, so he invented the electric razor. Marketed as the Schick Dry Shaver, it required nothing more than an electric socket to provide the perfect shave.

What's that humming sound? *Must be a bee...*

1929

Dyson vacuum cleaner

The first powered vacuum cleaner was designed by Herbert Booth in 1901. It was so big that it remained in the street while the cleaning was done using a long hose. In 1908, Hoover brought out an electric model based on an earlier design by James Spangler. The basic concept of sucking dust into a paper bag didn't change for over 80 years, until James Dyson released a bagless vacuum cleaner in 1993.

1993   1908   1901

Finding an alternative

The coal and oil that is burned to create steam and drive generators won't last for ever. Furthermore, burning these fossil fuels creates harmful "greenhouse gases" that may be causing global warming. So the race is on to find a practical, friendly alternative. Options include harnessing the power of the wind, waves, and tides.

What's that smell?

Greenhouse gas

Pardon me?

Someone's waving at me

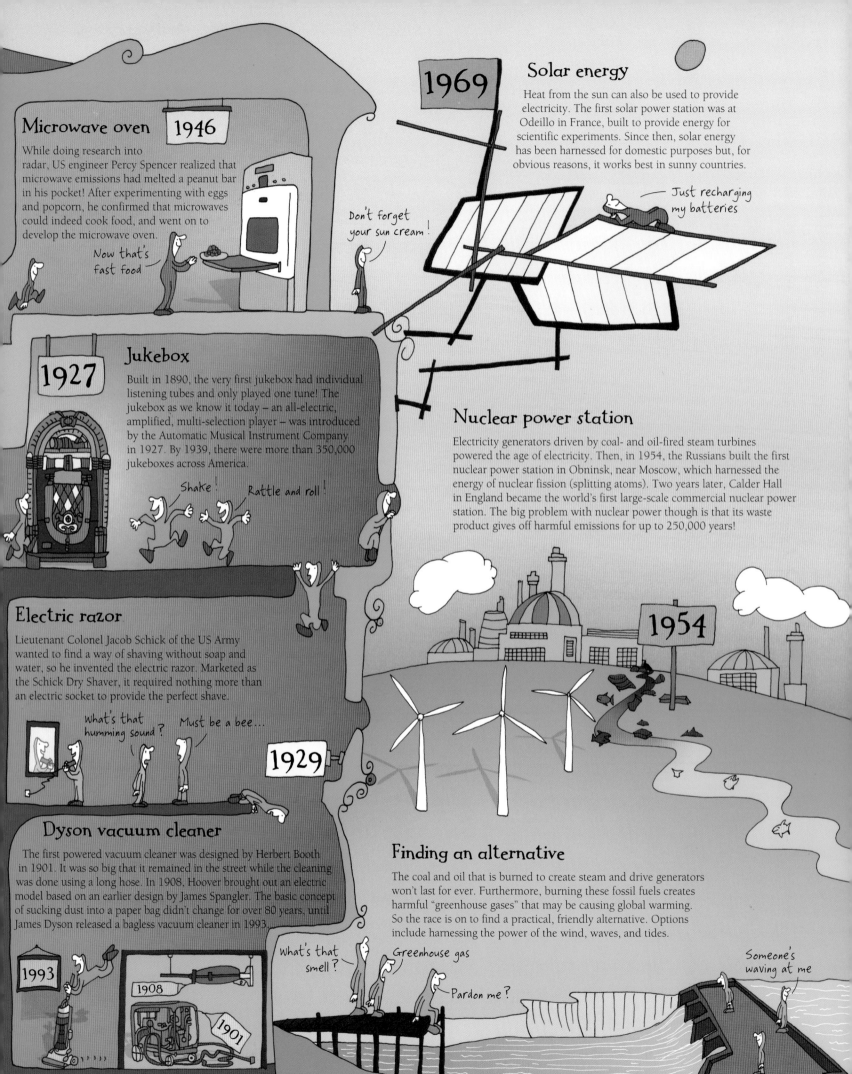

Washing machine

US engineer Alva Fisher mechanized the weekly wash by inventing the electric washing machine. Called Thor, it was little more than a wooden tub with an electric motor bolted underneath. Not surprisingly, washing machines weren't popular until the 1960s, when the first "twin tubs" appeared.

1907

Is there a wool wash?

Electric dishwasher

During the late 19th century, more than 30 women took out patents for dishwashers in the USA. The first machine to be manufactured was invented by Josephine Cochran, who had had enough of washing her own dishes. Initially powered by handle or steam engine, dishwashers didn't go electric until 1912. Even then, they didn't catch on in the home until the 1950s.

1912

Pop-up toaster

Burnt toast became commonplace once electric toasters had appeared on the breakfast table in 1893. In 1919, all that changed when American inventor Charles Strite patented the pop-up toaster. Originally designed for caterers, by 1926 it had reached the home in the form of the Toastmaster.

1919

Tuna   Beans Eggs Jam Honey

Peanut butter   Butter   Paté

I'll just pop up-stairs

You're toast!

1895 Electric drill

Having improved the design of the telephone, and invented the first electric fire alarm, German electrical engineer Wilhelm Fein went on to create the world's first electric hand drill.

Very handy

Electric refrigerator

In 1851, US doctor John Gorrie patented a refrigerator that relied on the expansion of a compressed gas (refrigerant) for its cooling effect. But refrigerators didn't go domestic until after 1913 when the first electric model was introduced, with a motorized compressor mounted on top that forced the refrigerant through metal coils.

1913

Motorized compressor   Indeed!

Cool

Electric hover-mower

1830

Lawnmowers date back to 1830 when Englishman Edwin Budding invented a machine with blades arranged around a cylinder. Nearly 100 years later the first electric models appeared. But the basic concept didn't change until the hover-mower was introduced in the 1960s, with rotary cutting blades replacing the cylinder.

1960s

Escalator

The escalator was invented by American engineer Jesse Reno. Called an inclined elevator, it was driven by an electric motor and had a continuous sloping belt instead of steps. It was so novel that, when one was fitted in London's famous Harrods department store in 1898, a man was on hand to dispense brandy to passengers overcome by the experience! Modern-style escalators with steps used a clever double wheel track system (see left), but they didn't appear until 1921.

KitchenAid

1916

More eggs!

Early food mixers were little more than motorized egg whisks. Then American engineer Herbert Johnson invented a new kind of multi-purpose mixer in which the beaters and bowl turned in opposite directions. Originally designed for the US Navy, within three years it was being sold to the public as the KitchenAid.

Hairdryer

Hand-held hairdryers were made possible thanks to the small, high-speed motors developed by American inventor Chester Beach in the early years of the 20th century. Containing a motorized fan that blew air over a heated element, early hairdryers were big, heavy, and noisy, with metal casing and a wooden handle.

Purrr....

Me next!

1920

Fascinating firsts

Have you ever wondered who invented sliced bread, when roller skates were first made, or how blue jeans came into existence? Even the most basic things we use every day, such as safety pins and tinned food, were invented by someone, sometime. Inventions such as false teeth may date back to Roman times, whereas others, like the artificial heart and the ejector seat, are very much a product of our modern age.

False teeth

The Etruscans, who ruled central Italy before the Romans, were the first to wear false teeth. They made them out of animal teeth held together by gold bridgework. Poor people couldn't afford false teeth, and had to cure the toothache with a mouthwash made by boiling dogs' teeth in wine!

Roller skates

The first roller skates on record were worn by a Belgian named Joseph Merlin, who sailed into a ballroom mounted on his skates and playing the violin. Alas, unable to stop or change his course, he crashed into a hideously expensive mirror and smashed it to smithereens!

Elastic band

Six years after the invention of vulcanized rubber, English rubber manufacturer Stephen Perry invented the elastic band as a means of holding bundles of papers together. It wasn't long before kids had found another use for the elastic band – firing projectiles at hapless friends and foe!

Safety pin

Where would we be without the safety pin? Clasp-type pins possibly date back to Roman times, but it was American inventor Walter Hunt who patented the design we still use today. As someone joked upon Hunt's death, "Without him we would be undone!"

Tinned food

The first patent for preserving food using "vessels of tin or other metals" was taken out by Englishman Peter Durand in 1810. Two years later, Bryan Donkin and John Hall set up the first canning factory to supply the army and navy with provisions. But the can-opener wasn't invented for another 43 years!

Jeans

When Californian tailor Jacob Davis was asked if he could design some work trousers with pockets that wouldn't keep tearing, he had the bright idea of using metal rivets on the pocket corners to take the strain. Before long he'd teamed up with denim supplier Levi Strauss, and Levi jeans were born!

Zip

The zip, or clasp locker as it was originally called, was invented by American engineer Whitcomb Judson as a device for doing up boots. But it had a major design fault – it kept coming undone! The modern style of zip was designed by Swedish engineer Gideon Sundback in 1913.

Traffic lights

The first electric traffic lights were installed at a road junction in Cleveland, USA, by the American Traffic Signal Company. But instead of having three lights, they comprised red and green only, plus a warning buzzer. The first three-colour traffic lights were installed in New York four years later.

Sliced bread

American jeweller Otto Frederick Rohwedder had something of an obsession with bread and spent 16 years perfecting his greatest invention – a bread-slicing machine. Sliced bread first went on sale in the small town of Chillicothe, Missouri. By 1933, 80 per cent of all bread sold in the USA was presliced.

Pilot ejector seat

The world's first ejector seat was fitted to an experimental German Heinkel jet fighter. Powered by compressed air, it proved its worth a few months later when it was used in a genuine emergency. The plane crashed but, thanks to the ejector seat, the pilot lived.

Disposable nappies

When American inventor Marion Davis came up with an idea for making leak-proof disposable nappies, her invention proved so popular she couldn't keep up with demand. So she sold the rights to a children's clothing manufacturer for $1 million and lived happily ever after!

Mouse

Many people had a hand in developing the computer, but the mouse was the brainchild of one person – US electronics engineer Douglas Engelbart. Patented as "an X-Y position indicator for a display system", its compact case and tail-like cable soon earned it its more endearing nickname.

Artificial heart

The human heart beats on average 2.5 billion times in a lifetime, so it's not surprising it sometimes goes wrong. The first successful artificial heart, the Jarvik-7, was designed by American doctor Robert Jarvik. When it was first used as a heart replacement in 1982, the patient survived an amazing 112 days.

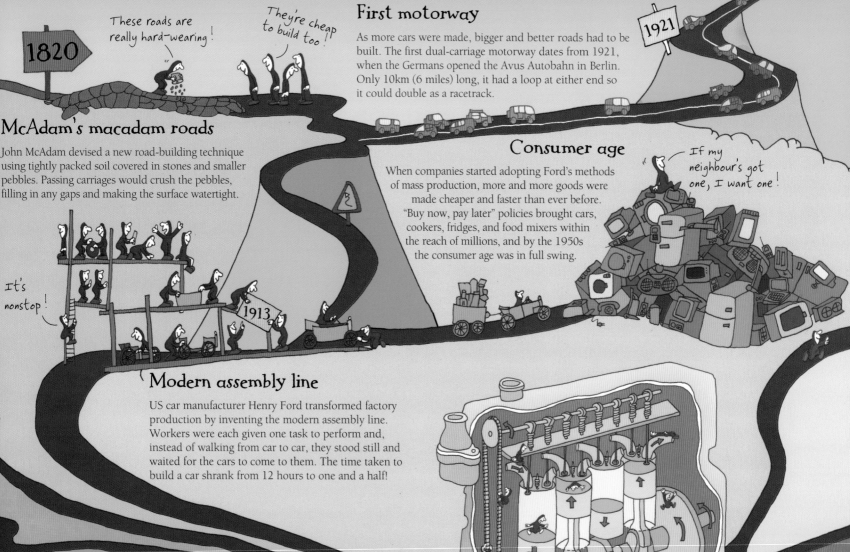

1820

"These roads are really hard-wearing!"

"They're cheap to build too!"

First motorway

1921

As more cars were made, bigger and better roads had to be built. The first dual-carriage motorway dates from 1921, when the Germans opened the Avus Autobahn in Berlin. Only 10km (6 miles) long, it had a loop at either end so it could double as a racetrack.

McAdam's macadam roads

John McAdam devised a new road-building technique using tightly packed soil covered in stones and smaller pebbles. Passing carriages would crush the pebbles, filling in any gaps and making the surface watertight.

Consumer age

When companies started adopting Ford's methods of mass production, more and more goods were made cheaper and faster than ever before. "Buy now, pay later" policies brought cars, cookers, fridges, and food mixers within the reach of millions, and by the 1950s the consumer age was in full swing.

"If my neighbour's got one, I want one!"

"It's nonstop!"

1913

Modern assembly line

US car manufacturer Henry Ford transformed factory production by inventing the modern assembly line. Workers were each given one task to perform and, instead of walking from car to car, they stood still and waited for the cars to come to them. The time taken to build a car shrank from 12 hours to one and a half!

Otto cycle

In 1876, German engineer Nikolaus Otto invented the engine cycle that still bears his name. Alphonse Beau de Rochas had first described a four-stroke cycle in 1862, but Otto reinvented it, and was soon putting it to the test in his new line of gas engines.

"Did I hear someone invented a bike with an engine?"

Motorbike

When Gottlieb Daimler developed the petrol engine, instead of putting it straight onto a carriage, he built a wooden bike and tested it on that. He'd just invented the motorbike! But it was nine years before motorbikes went into production.

"Hey, he's not pedalling up there!"

1885

By land, sea, and air

Many inventions contributed to the success of the motor car and the petrol engine, from wheels and roads to turret lathes and petrol pumps. But there was more to come. In 1892, Rudolf Diesel invented a new kind of internal combustion engine, ideal for powering heavy machinery, ships, and locomotives. In 1903, the Wright brothers took to the skies. And by 1937, Frank Whittle had built the world's first jet engine, giving rise to a new age in air transport.

It all began here 5,500 years ago

I've invented the wheel!

The wheel

Wheels were first used in Mesopotamia (now Iraq) around 3500BC. We know about them through ancient pictograms (picture writing). They probably developed from rollers made from tree trunks, used for moving heavy objects. Although wheels were soon widespread, some people, such as the Aztecs, never found out about them.

Roman roads

Not surprisingly, roads date back as far as the wheel, to ancient Mesopotamia. But it was the Ancient Romans who perfected the art of road building, constructing a network of more than 80,000km (50,000 miles) of roads across their vast empire.

Pointless!

Wonderful!

AD200

Great for marching on!

Pneumatic tyre

Robert Thompson invented a pneumatic, or air-filled, tyre in 1845. But it was soon forgotten. Forty-two years later, Scottish vet John Dunlop reinvented it while trying to improve the ride on his son's tricycle using a rubber garden hose.

Arrgh, it's sticky!

1839

Much better!

1887

I've just invented the puncture — No!

Vulcanization

Charles Goodyear invented a way of "curing" rubber to stop it getting tacky in summer and brittle in winter. Called vulcanization, it made rubber stronger and harder without reducing its elasticity. Soon rubber was being used for making shoes, fans, tyres, toys, balls, and many other items. Alas, Goodyear's invention did not make him rich – he died a poor man, deeply in debt.

Tools

Tools

More tools

19th century

Nut house

New tools

Inventions such as Fitch's turret lathe and Baker and Holt's ball-grinding machine paved the way for the motor car and mass production, by enabling thousands of identical parts for engines and other machines to be made faster and more accurately than ever before.

Single cylinder engine

Designed and built by Belgian engineer Étienne Lenoir in 1859, the first successful internal combustion engine had a single cylinder and ran on gas. Despite its large size, it was rather feeble and only managed two horsepower. Nonetheless, in 1862, Lenoir fixed it to an old horse cart and took it for a 10-km (6-mile) spin.

It's a gas!

Steam power

The steam engine had powered a revolution in industry and transport, but it was too impractical ever to change the course of road travel. That awaited the invention of a more practical engine that was easier to start – namely, the internal combustion engine.

18th century

1859

Petrol pump

When anxious storekeeper Jake Gumper asked Sylvanus J Bowser to help stop a leaking paraffin barrel from tainting his butter cask, he got the world's first petrol pump! Bowser's remedy was to design a special dispenser with a pump handle that meted out given quantities of oil. Within 20 years, Bowser's pump was dispensing petrol for motor cars.

Up with pedal power

First oil well

Edwin Drake set out to drill for oil in Titusville, Pennsylvania, employing the same methods as used for boring salt water. When oil started flooding out of the bore hole, Drake quickly attached a hand pump and became the first person to pump oil from a well!

where's the oil?

Looks useful!

Do you take credit cards?

1885

1859

Drill engine

Drilling tool

Iron pipe inserted underground

On the road

The steam engine had powered a revolution in industry and transport. But, although it rivalled the petrol engine for more than 20 years, it was too impractical, and took too long to get started, ever to become master of the roads. Beginning life as a stationary engine for driving industrial machinery, it was the internal combustion engine that caused the transport revolution of the 20th century, evolving into a light and highly efficient machine that made the motor car the "must-have" mode of transport for the masses.

Into the future

Driven men
Karl Benz and Gottlieb Daimler competed against each other in the development of the motor car.

First car
1885
Karl Benz built the first successful motor car in 1885. It was powered by petrol engine and steered by a tiller, but only had three wheels!

The internal combustion engine

The first internal combustion engines ran on coal gas. Then, in 1885, German engineers Gottlieb Daimler and Wilhelm Maybach developed a successful petrol engine. With a single cylinder that operated on a four-stroke cycle (see right), the engine soon evolved into the four-cylinder type that is still used in cars today. The power comes from burning fuel inside the cylinders, which drives the pistons down and turns the crankshaft.

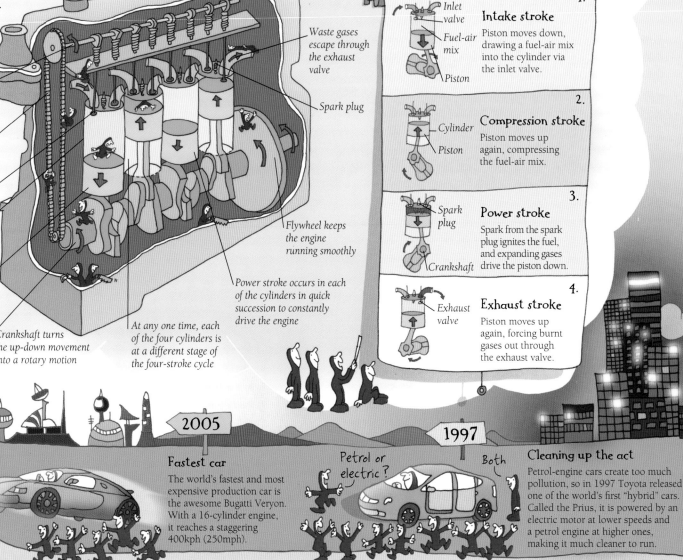

Overhead camshaft controls the opening and closing of the valves

Camdrive belt, driven by the crankshaft, turns the overhead camshaft

Inlet valve
Cylinders contain close-fitting pistons

Piston in each cylinder moves up and down, turning the crankshaft with every power stroke

Crankshaft turns the up-down movement into a rotary motion

At any one time, each of the four cylinders is at a different stage of the four-stroke cycle

Waste gases escape through the exhaust valve

Spark plug

Flywheel keeps the engine running smoothly

Power stroke occurs in each of the cylinders in quick succession to constantly drive the engine

Four-stroke cycle

When the engine is running, each cylinder continuously performs a cycle of four events, called the four-stroke cycle. The events occur in sequence across the four cylinders, so that as one cylinder is carrying out the intake stroke, the next is completing the compression stroke, and so on.

1.
Inlet valve
Fuel-air mix
Piston
Intake stroke
Piston moves down, drawing a fuel-air mix into the cylinder via the inlet valve.

2.
Cylinder
Piston
Compression stroke
Piston moves up again, compressing the fuel-air mix.

3.
Spark plug
Crankshaft
Power stroke
Spark from the spark plug ignites the fuel, and expanding gases drive the piston down.

4.
Exhaust valve
Exhaust stroke
Piston moves up again, forcing burnt gases out through the exhaust valve.

Fastest car
2005
The world's fastest and most expensive production car is the awesome Bugatti Veyron. With a 16-cylinder engine, it reaches a staggering 400kph (250mph).

Petrol or electric?
Both

Cleaning up the act
1997
Petrol-engine cars create too much pollution, so in 1997 Toyota released one of the world's first "hybrid" cars. Called the Prius, it is powered by an electric motor at lower speeds and a petrol engine at higher ones, making it much cleaner to run.

The first "modern" motor car

The Panhard Levassor of 1891 was the first "modern" motor car. It had several features in common with today's cars – a front-mounted engine, pedal-operated clutch, central gearbox, and rear-wheel drive – but still lacked many things that we now take for granted.

Front-mounted engine

Tiller

Before starter motors were invented, people had to crank a heavy starting handle to get a car started. It was hard work!

Wooden wheels

Chain

Gearbox control lever

So heavy!

*The Panhard Levassor was the first car to have the **engine mounted at the front** instead of the back. The extra weight over the front wheels made the car easier to steer.*

Blinding!

*Early cars used candle-lit carriage lamps for lighting. The first **electric lamps** were fitted in 1908.*

*Early cars were steered by a tiller. But **steering wheels** weren't far around the corner – the first one was fitted in 1894.*

Is it a pogo stick?

*The first **drive shaft** was fitted to a Renault in 1898. Before that, the wheels were driven by a chain, rather like a bicycle!*

Music to my ears!

Car radios *were first fitted in 1927, not long after radio broadcasting began.*

What a bright spark!

Spark plugs *were invented in 1902 by German engineer Gottlob Honold.*

Jumper! *Bumper!*

*The first **bumper** was fitted to a Czech-built car in 1897, but it fell off after about 15km (9 miles) and no-one bothered to replace it!*

First four-wheeler

The following year, Gottlieb Daimler built the first four-wheel car but, rather than start from scratch, he simply added a petrol engine to a horse-drawn carriage!

So much smoother with four wheels

Wow, 3 wheels! *And so fast!*

1886

1896

Stop!

*Early wheels were made of wood, sometimes with solid rubber tyres. The Michelin brothers fitted the first **pneumatic tyres** in 1895, giving a much softer ride!*

What a way to go

It wasn't long before the motor car claimed its first victim. In 1896, poor old Mrs Bridget Driscoll was killed by a joy-rider at Crystal Palace, London. And the car was only travelling at 6kph (4mph)!

She's dead!

Oops!

I told you to slow down

It's nice and dry in here

*An 1898 Renault became the first car to have an **enclosed cabin**.*

Quick start

The first car to be fitted with an electric starter motor was the British Arnold, back in 1896. But starter motors didn't catch on until 1912, when the US firm Cadillac began fitting them as standard.

1912

Rotary engine cars

The 1964 NSU Spider was the first car to be powered by a rotary engine. Invented by Felix Wankel in 1958, this engine has moving parts that go round and round, instead of up and down like a piston engine.

Woof!

Noisy isn't it! *What?* *Shhh!*

Diesel-engine cars

The first production car powered by a diesel engine was built by Mercedes-Benz in 1936. It used a lot less fuel than a petrol-engine car, making it cheaper to run, but it was much noisier!

1936

Helicopter

German professor Heinrich Focke built the first practical helicopter. Instead of having a single rotor, like today's helicopters, it had two that turned in opposite directions. Russian-born US engineer Igor Sikorsky built the first single-rotor helicopter in 1939.

1936

Super!

Sonic!

1976

Concorde

With its streamlined body, delta wings, and adjustable nose, Concorde was the world's first – and only – supersonic airliner. It cruised at an amazing 2,125kph (1,320mph), and made a characteristic "boom" as it zoomed through the air faster than the speed of sound.

First jet

Working along similar lines to Whittle, German physicist Hans Joachim Pabst von Ohain designed the jet engine that powered the world's first jet aircraft – the experimental Heinkel He 178.

1939

I'm feeling flushed

1952

Are we nearly there yet?

Don't look down!

Passenger jets

The world's first jet airliner was the British de Havilland Comet. With a cruising speed of 800kph (500mph), it halved flying times between major cities. But it was plagued with accidents and, by 1958, had lost its lead to the American Boeing 707.

Flying bedstead

Nicknamed the flying bedstead for obvious reasons, Rolls-Royce's experimental "Thrust Measuring Rig" became the world's first vertical take-off jet-powered machine. Its technology was used to develop the Harrier "jump jet".

1954

Jump jet

The British Harrier "jump jet" was the first jet aircraft capable of taking off vertically. It does so by directing its jets downwards instead of backwards. The Harrier is so versatile that it can even fly backwards!

1966

Hovercraft

After testing his theories with two tin cans and a vacuum cleaner that blew instead of sucked air, Christopher Cockerel went on to invent the hovercraft. Riding on a cushion of air to reduce friction, his new machine could travel across both land and water.

1955

Help!

Jump!

This thing's melting

Downward air flow pushes the hovercraft upward

Lifting fan draws air downward

Global warming

Today, we have more cars, planes, and consumer goods than ever before. But by burning fossil fuels – petrol, gas, and oil – to run cars and manufacture goods we are creating too many harmful "greenhouse" gases and things are going haywire! Floods, droughts, famine, and melting ice caps are a high price to pay.

Up, up and away

A duck, a rooster, and a sheep became the first-ever aircraft passengers when they took to the skies over France in the Montgolfier brothers' hot-air balloon. Two months later, the first humans were airborne.

1783

look up

1853

Cayley's glider

British baron Sir George Cayley was the first person to work out the principles of aerodynamics (what makes things fly). At the age of 80, he also built the world's first successful glider. But, rather than test it himself, he sent his coachman up instead. After making the first manned flight in a heavier-than-air craft, his coachman tried to quit, saying he was hired to drive, not fly!

I resign!

I feel revolting!

It's a revolution

1903

1933

Boeing 247

Early airliners were mostly biplanes, with two sets of wings. The first ones were converted World War I bombers but, by the 1920s, specially designed models were being built to meet growing demand. The first "modern" airliner was the 1933 Boeing 247 – an all-metal, low-wing monoplane that carried 10 passengers and cruised at 250kph (155mph).

First flight

On 17 December 1903, in North Carolina, USA, brothers Wilbur and Orville Wright made the world's first successful flights in a heavier-than-air powered aircraft. Their longest flight that day, in their *Flyer Number 1*, lasted only 59 seconds and covered just 260m (853ft), but it was enough to start a transport revolution.

1930

Jet engine

In 1930, English engineer Frank Whittle designed a new kind of engine that used the rotary motion of a turbine to create a powerful rush, or "jet", of hot gases, which could push an aeroplane forward at great speed. Whittle built his first test engine in 1937 but, before he could fit it to an aircraft, Germany had beaten him to it!

Diesel engine

German engineer Rudolf Diesel designed a new type of engine that relied on highly compressed hot air, instead of spark plugs, to spontaneously ignite the fuel. Noisy and heavy, but cheaper to run than a petrol engine, it was first put to work in a brewery in St Louis, USA.

Motor boat

In their early days, petrol engines were considered to be dangerous. So when Gottlieb Daimler demonstrated the world's first petrol-driven motor boat, he added lots of wires to fool people into thinking it was powered by electricity.

Excellent for fishing

1892

Cheers!

Fine machines these diesel engines!

Is it a bird?

or a boat?

1886

Fabulous flops

As Edison once said, "I have failed my way to success!" And, indeed, flops form part of the process of invention, helping to drive people on to greater things. Some inventions, such as Garnerin's parachute, have technical hitches that are later ironed out; others, like Hughes's gigantic Spruce Goose, are overambitious and doomed to failure from the start. Then there are inventions like Sinclair's C5 electric car that fail simply because no-one wants them in the first place!

oh dear

1801

Captain Dick's Puffer

Richard Trevithick is famous for inventing the steam locomotive. But things didn't go too well when he took his first passenger steam carriage, Captain Dick's Puffer, out for a spin. He left it running while he went inside an inn to celebrate his success and the engine blew up!

Next, I'll invent a sick bag

1894

More wings maybe?

1797

I'm not feeling well

First parachute jump

Frenchman André Garnerin built himself a 7m- (23ft-) wide canopy out of canvas and made the first-ever parachute jump, leaping from a hydrogen balloon. The trouble was, he didn't know to cut a hole in the top to let the air through, and the parachute swung so wildly he was violently sick. But at least he landed safely!

Maxim's flying machine

Inventor of the machine gun, Hiram Maxim built a massive flying machine that ran on rails for take-off. With five pairs of wings spanning 38m (125ft), and two gasoline-powered steam engines driving a pair of huge propellers, it briefly took flight before crashing to the ground in a crumpled heap.

Edison's failures

Despite some spectacular successes, Thomas Edison also had some disastrous failures. One was his attempt to build furniture out of "foam concrete". Another cost him his entire fortune when he invested, unsuccessfully, in a new technique for extracting iron from low-grade ore using magnets.

c1890–1910

Amphicar

Advertised as "the car that swims", the Amphicar was the brainchild of German designer Hans Trippel. It combined the features of a boat and a car, but on land it was like a fish out of water, happiest at a slothful 65kph (40mph). Not surprisingly, the idea didn't catch on!

APT

Designed to tilt as it went round corners, British Rail's pioneering new Advanced Passenger Train was plagued with problems right from the start, including the fact that it made passengers feel sick! After seven years of costly development, the whole project was scrapped.

We're sunk

1961

1982

Yikes!

Aerial steam carriage

1843

British engineer William Henson's aerial steam carriage had much to recommend it. Powered by steam, it was the world's first aircraft to have a fixed, wire-braced monowing and to be driven by propeller. The only problem was, it was just too heavy to fly!

It flies... almost!

De Groof parachute

1874

I'm heading south for the winter

Belgian Vincent de Groof's big ambition was to fly like a bird. So he built himself a parachute machine with bird-like wings that he hitched to a balloon to be carried aloft over London. But when he released his apparatus, the wings collapsed and de Groof came crashing to the ground. His flying days were over before they'd begun!

Spruce Goose

When billionaire Howard Hughes built the world's biggest aircraft, he also created one of the biggest-ever flops. Nicknamed "Spruce Goose" by the press in reference to its wooden frame and clumsy take-off, his gigantic flying boat was too big for its own good and only flew the once.

1947

Should spruce things up a bit

Rocking saloon ship

1874

I'm sick of this

Famous for inventing an efficient way of making steel, British inventor Henry Bessemer was not so successful when it came to inventing ships. He built a steamer with a rocking saloon, designed to swing in a a swell and prevent seasickness. Alas, it lurched more violently and made people more sick than ever!

Sinclair C5

British inventor Clive Sinclair intended his C5 electric vehicle as a cheap, clean alternative to gas-guzzling motorcars. But, powered by the kind of motor used in washing machines, with pedals for going uphill and a top speed of only 24kph (15mph), it's not surprising the C5 wasn't a great hit!

1985

Let's go for a spin

Nimslo 3-D camera

1980s

Say cheese

In the past, 3-D photography had always required a special viewer. Then Jerry Nims and Allen Lo invented an ingenious camera that took four frames per shot and produced a single 3-D print. But their Nimslo camera cost up to 10 times more than a normal one and never took off.

Hunley submarine

The world's first submarine attack was both a success and a failure. During the American Civil War, Horace Hunley built a submarine based on an old boiler and armed it with a torpedo strapped to the end of a long spar. The vessel succeeded in sinking an enemy ship but blew itself up at the same time, killing all on board!

1864

Hello!

Magnetic recording

1898

In designing the first telephone answering machine, Danish telephone engineer Valdemar Poulsen invented a new way of recording sound, using magnetism. He made recordings by magnetizing piano wire, but the technology didn't really take off until the 1930s, when the first modern tape recorder was invented using plastic tape.

Any messages for me?

Super sound

1960

Careful!

Laser

Just as transistors were designed to amplify electronic signals, so lasers were designed to amplify light. US physicist Theodore Maiman built the first working laser, producing an intense beam of pure light in which the waves were all in step with each other. Within a few years lasers had been put to work in surgery, surveying, metal cutting, and holograms.

Berliner gramophone

It was German engineer Emile Berliner who switched from using cylinders to flat disks for recording sound. The forerunner of the more modern record player, his gramophone produced better sound than Edison's phonograph and soon records were being mass-produced in their thousands.

1888

Terrific

1906

I'm on top of my workload

Let's all communicate

The transistor not only transformed computer technology, it revolutionized entertainment and communications as well. By packing the power of its predecessor – the triode valve – into a tiny component, it gave rise to a host of smaller, cheaper devices, from transistor radios to portable television sets, and record players. And as it shrunk still further in size, becoming the essential component of microchips, it went on to shape the world we know today.

Triode valve

When US inventor Lee De Forest invented the triode valve, it heralded the dawn of the age of electronics. Looking rather like a light bulb, it was designed to detect radio waves and control electric current. Later, valves came into their own boosting radio and television signals, amplifying sound in record players, and acting as "switches" in computers.

1935

Radar

Scottish engineer Robert Watson-Watt employed valves in his "radio detection and ranging" system. Better known as radar, it involved bouncing radio waves off enemy aircraft and using the echo to pinpoint the aircraft's distance.

1954

Transistor radio

Early radio sets were large and clumsy, and used a device called a "cat's whisker" or, later, valves to receive radio signals. But with the invention of the transistor, small portable radios became feasible. The first transistor radio was the American Regency TR1 – small enough to fit in a pocket.

Semaphore telegraph

1791

What did you say?

Since ancient times people have used smoke signals and drums to send simple messages. The Romans were the first to devise a system of flag waving to spell out words. Then, in 1791, Frenchman Claude Chappé updated the idea by inventing the semaphore telegraph. This comprised a network of wooden posts with hinged "arms" for sending coded messages over long distances.

Edison phonograph

1877

Whilst seeking ways of recording telegraph messages, American invento[r] Thomas Edison came up with one of h[is] greatest inventions – the phonograph. Sound was recorded using a needle vibrating against a revolving cylinder wrapped in tin foil. For playback, the process was simply repeated, and the vibrations transformed back into sound.

Electric telegraph

1837

Communications were revolutionized when British inventors William Cooke and Charles Wheatstone devised a way of sending messages using electric signals. Their telegraph machine had five needles pointing to 20 letters of the alphabet, so it was hard luck if you wanted to send words with Q, X, or Z!

Microphone

1878

What's that stomping?

English music professor David Hughes is credited with inventing the first truly effective microphone. Made up of three ordinary nails and some loose wire, his experimental model was so sensitive it could detect a fly's footstep.

Radio broadcasting

1920s

It was a big step from wireless telegraphy to broadcasting music and speech over the airwaves. American Reginald Fessenden made the first advertised radio broadcast on Christmas Eve, 1906. By the mid-1920s, public broadcasting was becoming all the rage, with people eagerly tuning in on their new wireless sets.

Music to my ears

Wireless telegraphy

1894

My go!

What's it saying?

Sssss!

Snakes?

The electric telegraph relied on wires to transmit coded messages. Then Italian inventor Guglielmo Marconi invented a way of sending telegraph signals through the air using radio waves instead of electricity. In 1901, he managed to send the first wireless telegraph message across the Atlantic – it was the letter "S"!

Telephone

1876

Hello

Hello

It speaks!

Electric telegraphy was ideal for sending coded messages over long distances. But Scottish-born inventor Alexander Graham Bell wanted to find a way of transmitting speech. The result was the telephone, in which electrical signals imitate the vibrations of the human voice.

Super-duper computer

Mechanical calculating machines have been around for more than 350 years. But, following the invention of a device called a "triode valve" in the early 20th century, a new type of calculator was born – the electronic computer. Computers differ from calculators in that they are programmable – that is, they have a memory and can store instructions. Early computers had thousands of valves and took up entire rooms. Then, in 1947, three scientists invented something very small that was to have a very big impact on all our lives – the transistor.

Terrific

Amazing

The transistor

Set the task of improving the telephone system, a team of scientists at Bell Telephone Laboratories in the USA transformed electronics by inventing the transistor. It did the work of a triode valve, amplifying electrical signals and acting as a "switch" in computers, but was very much smaller and more reliable. As transistors replaced valves, computers got smaller and cheaper, and their numbers exploded.

These things seem to be multiplying!

Portraits

John Bardeen

William Shockley

Walter Brattain

US physicists John Bardeen, Walter Brattain, and William Shockley invented the transistor in 1947 and were awarded a Nobel Prize for their outstanding work.

Pascal's calculator

1642

A taxing invention

French physicist and mathematician Blaise Pascal built an elaborate calculator for his father, who was a tax inspector. Comprising a series of dials and gears, it could only do addition, and even then it wasn't very reliable!

Babbage's analytical engine

1834

You seen my hole puncher?

Mathematician Charles Babbage designed the world's first mechanical computer. Called an analytical engine, it would have been enormous, powered by steam engine and programmed using punched cards. But only a small section was ever built.

Binary computer

1940

11001O0 110010 ?

O1011O11 O11O11110 !

1001

US mathematicians John Atanasoff and Clifford Berry tried to build the first electronic computer based on the binary system. Although they never finished their ABC machine, binary became the basis for all future computers.

Electronic computer

1944

What is it?

A secret

During World War II, British engineer Tommy Flowers built the first-ever electronic computer, designed to break enemy codes. Containing 1,800 valves, his Colossus machine was so secret that, for 50 years, hardly anyone knew it existed!

Computers at home

A modern home computer system is made up of many internal and external elements all linked together, each with its own function. Some elements, such as the keyboard, CD-ROM drive, and microphone, are designed to input information, or data, into the computer; others, such as the microprocessor, graphics card, and RAM, are designed to process or store the data. The screen and printer are known as output units, displaying the end results of a computer's task.

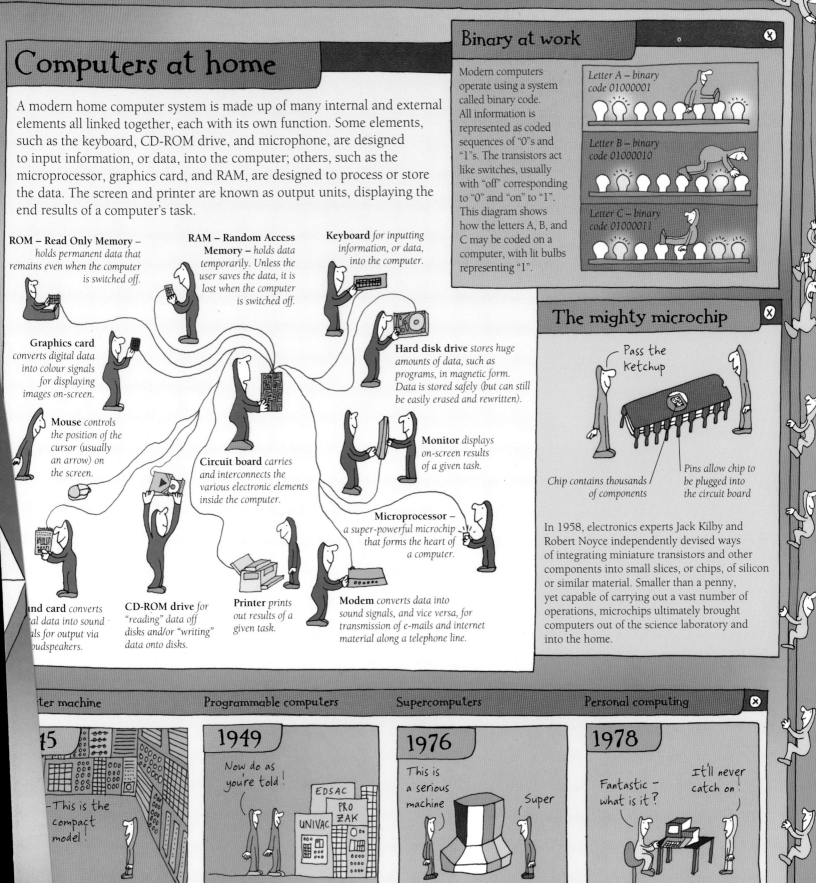

ROM – Read Only Memory – *holds permanent data that remains even when the computer is switched off.*

RAM – Random Access Memory – *holds data temporarily. Unless the user saves the data, it is lost when the computer is switched off.*

Keyboard *for inputting information, or data, into the computer.*

Graphics card *converts digital data into colour signals for displaying images on-screen.*

Hard disk drive *stores huge amounts of data, such as programs, in magnetic form. Data is stored safely (but can still be easily erased and rewritten).*

Mouse *controls the position of the cursor (usually an arrow) on the screen.*

Circuit board *carries and interconnects the various electronic elements inside the computer.*

Monitor *displays on-screen results of a given task.*

Microprocessor – *a super-powerful microchip that forms the heart of a computer.*

Sound card *converts digital data into sound signals for output via loudspeakers.*

CD-ROM drive *for "reading" data off disks and/or "writing" data onto disks.*

Printer *prints out results of a given task.*

Modem *converts data into sound signals, and vice versa, for transmission of e-mails and internet material along a telephone line.*

Binary at work

Modern computers operate using a system called binary code. All information is represented as coded sequences of "0"s and "1"s. The transistors act like switches, usually with "off" corresponding to "0" and "on" to "1". This diagram shows how the letters A, B, and C may be coded on a computer, with lit bulbs representing "1".

Letter A – binary code 01000001

Letter B – binary code 01000010

Letter C – binary code 01000011

The mighty microchip

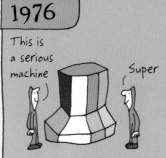

Pass the Ketchup

Chip contains thousands of components

Pins allow chip to be plugged into the circuit board

In 1958, electronics experts Jack Kilby and Robert Noyce independently devised ways of integrating miniature transistors and other components into small slices, or chips, of silicon or similar material. Smaller than a penny, yet capable of carrying out a vast number of operations, microchips ultimately brought computers out of the science laboratory and into the home.

...ter machine

...15

—This is the compact model!

...nown" electronic computer was ...C. Built by US scientists to do ...e military, it had over 18,000 ...hed as much as six elephants, ...a whole room. Even so, in ...s it wasn't very fast!

Programmable computers

1949

Now do as you're told!

EDSAC

PRO ZAK

UNIVAC

Early machines weren't "real" computers because they could not be programmed (store instructions). The first to do so was called EDSAC, built by a team at Cambridge University, England. The Americans soon followed with BINAC and UNIVAC computers.

Supercomputers

1976

This is a serious machine

Super

Really serious mathematics requires really serious computers. The Cray-1 was the first of a new generation of "supercomputers", designed by US engineer Seymour Cray to carry out upwards of 240 million calculations per second.

Personal computing

1978

Fantastic – what is it?

It'll never catch on!

Small desktop computers only became possible with the invention of the microprocessor. The first successful one, complete with keyboard and screen, was the Apple II, designed by US techies Steve Jobs and Steve Wozniak.

Video game

1972

The world's first successful video game was invented by US computer buff Nolan Bushnell. Called Pong, it consisted of two paddles knocking a ball back and forth!

1972

Freewheeling robot

Microchips were ideal for bringing robots to life. Industrial robots date from 1961, but the first mobile robot was the aptly-named Shakey – a US research machine from 1972 that was far from steady on its wheels!

1983

I've got junk mail

The Internet

Until the 1960s, computers could only "talk" to each other on a one-to-one basis via, for example, a telephone link. Then a new system – called packet switching – was invented, enabling several computers to communicate across a network. Over the years, networks grew larger and multiplied across the world until, in 1983, a standardized method of communication was adopted, called TCP/IP, and the Internet was born.

Television broadcasting

Back in Britain, the BBC started the first public television broadcasting service, pitting Baird's mechanical system against an electronic one. There was no competition and within three months Baird's system had been dropped.

1936

I'm on telly!

Lunokhod

1970

Terrific view

Deep in space, robots are better equipped than humans to cope with their strange surroundings. The first robot to land on the Moon was the Russian *Lunokhod* explorer. Powered by solar panels, it was able to roam freely, taking photographs and relaying them back to Earth by radio.

Where on Earth am I?

A shrinking world

Today, thanks to modern electronics, a vast global pool of information can be accessed at the touch of a button, live TV broadcasts can be beamed from one side of the world to another, and people in even the remotest areas can communicate instantly with loved ones far away. Distance is no longer a barrier to communication and the world seems to be shrinking!

Yikes, it's shrinking!

1962

Telstar

US engineer John Pierce showed that radio signals could be transmitted across vast distances by bouncing them off a satellite. *Telstar* tested his ideas and became the first satellite to relay television broadcasts across the Atlantic.

1990s

Let's shop!

Chip and pin

Today, microchips have transformed the way we shop. In an effort to cut crime, most bank cards now incorporate a microchip that stores information about a person's PIN, or personal identity number. When someone buys goods, instead of signing for them, they simply tap their PIN into a small machine and it's checked against the number stored on the card.

1982

Compact disc player

Electronics giants Sony and Philips pooled resources to invent a new kind of music playback system – the compact disc player. Making full use of laser technology, sound information is stored as a series of pits on the surface of the disk and played back using a laser beam.

It's the pits

1998

MP3 player

The latest way to buy music is to download it from the Internet, using a compression system called MP3. Developed by the Fraunhofer Institut in Germany, MP3 can shrink an audio file down to one-twelfth of its size with little loss of quality.

Microchips and microprocessors

The next big leap forward in electronics was the invention in 1958 of the microchip, followed in 1971 by the more powerful microprocessor. Not only were TVs, radios, and computers transformed yet again, but a host of new devices such as mobile phones, digital cameras, and CD players also came on the scene. Today, everything from washing machines to motorcars contains a microprocessor!

1958

I've got a transistor blister

Help!

There it is

Great pins!

My stuff's getting smaller

Can't resist a transistor

1947

1979

Mobile phone

Phones went wireless when the Bell Telephone Laboratories developed the "cellular" system for transmitting calls by radio wave. This involved setting up a network of small areas, or cells, each with its own localized transmitter. The trouble was, early mobile phones were so big they were too heavy to carry around. But they gradually got smaller, going digital in 1991.

1897

Cathode ray tube

German physicist Ferdinand Braun invented a device for moving a beam of electrons across a screen coated with phosphorescent powder. Where the beam hit the screen the powder glowed, creating patterns of light. Thirty years on, his "cathode ray tube" would form the basis of electronic television.

1926

Baird television

Scottish inventor John Logie Baird was the first to demonstrate television, using a series of spinning disks to transmit an image of a ventriloquist's dummy. His device was mechanical, rather than electronic, and was doomed to be overtaken by developments in America and Britain.

1928

Electronic television

Television was pioneered in America by self-taught whizz kid Philo T Farnsworth. He gave the first demonstration of an all-electronic television system, complete with valves and cathode ray tube.

THE FUTURE

And what of the Future? We can get some clue to what it promises by looking at ideas currently being developed, such as growing organs for transplant, harnessing nuclear fusion for pollution-free energy, and building hotels in space. But some concepts, such as travelling through time and making contact with alien life forms, are still so remote that they belong more to works of fiction than to any realistic vision of the future.

Fuel cells

The idea of combining hydrogen with oxygen to make water and release energy dates back to 1839, when Welsh judge William Grove designed the first fuel cell. Since then, fuel cells have been much improved and successfully used to power space flights. But, more importantly, they could help solve our energy crisis by providing pollution-free power for the motorcar.

Perfect evening

No fumes!

Solar cars

In 1990, Australia staged the first World Solar Challenge, in which solar cars competed in a 3,000km (1,864 mile) journey across the continent. The most recent winner was Nuno 3, the first to achieve an average speed of more than 100kph (62mph). But, if solar cars represent the future of motoring, nobody's going to get very far on a cloudy day!

No cloudy days in space!

You've made tiny versions of everything? *Yes, but now I can't find them...*

Watch the fingers!

Let's moonwalk

Nanotechnology

The latest thing in electronics is "nanotechnology" – that is, technology that works on a scale of one billionth (1,000,000,000th) of a metre. It involves creating minuscule machines out of individual molecules that, one day, may be used to fight disease, clean up pollution, and make enough food to feed the world.

Help!

Hang on

Let's go to 1967

Space hotels

Space tourism is already a reality, with some companies aiming to build hotels in space by the year 2020. Shaped like ring doughnuts, such hotels would spin round a central axis to create a sense of gravity in space.

Time travel

According to Einstein, time slows down the faster you travel, and stops altogether when you reach the speed of light. In theory, this means that, by travelling faster than the speed of light, you could go backwards in time. But, as we can only travel at a fraction of light speed, time travel may be a very long way off!

I wonder how many stars this hotel has

Silent aircraft

Twenty years from now, noisy aircraft may be a thing of the past. Cambridge University and the Massachusetts Institute of Technology have joined forces to design a new generation of aircraft that will be so quiet that no-one will hear them outside an airport.

Implanting ideas

One day, microprocessor implants buried under the skin may transmit information to sensors and computers all around us. They would help make our lives easier, unlocking our front doors when we get home, turning our computers on as we sit down, and paying for things without cards or money. They may even transmit thoughts and feelings to other people!

This chip under my skin activates the toaster

Robot helper

Robotic vacuum cleaners have been around since 2001, but the likelihood of robotic humanoids helping in the home is still a long way off. Just keeping a two-legged robot upright requires some highly complex technology, let alone having it make a cup of coffee!

What is your bidding master?

Can you wash the dishes?

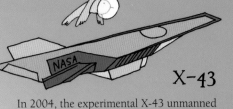

X-43

In 2004, the experimental X-43 unmanned hypersonic aircraft made its first test flight, reaching the astonishing speed of Mach 7 (that is, seven times the speed of sound). This might represent air transport of the future, capable of whizzing us to any destination on Earth in under two hours.

You think aliens are watching us right now?

I doubt it!

I reckon it's fused!

Flibble wibble!

Is anyone out there?

Even as you read this, tracking stations using powerful radio telescopes are scanning the cosmos for signs of extraterrestrial life. We may already have the technology to find alien life forms, but will we have the technology to reach them once we've found them?

Fuel shortage

We're running out of fossil fuels and, unless a safe alternative is found soon, the future may be a lot less hi-tech than we imagine! One option under investigation is nuclear fusion. Unlike nuclear *fission*, which is used today in power stations and produces harmful waste products, nuclear *fusion* (fusing two atomic nuclei) would produce the harmless gas helium.

Wearing your heart on your sleeve again?

Growing organs

Cloning human beings may not be acceptable, but some scientists believe that using cloning techniques to grow human organs may be the way of the future. It would mean, for example, if someone had a dodgy kidney, scientists could simply grow a new one and replace it!

Human cloning

An exact replica of another sheep, Dolly became the world's first cloned animal in 1997. Research into cloning humans, however, is considered wrong and is banned in many countries. But that's not to say it won't happen some time in the future.

We look the same?

No, we don't

Yes, we do!

Baaaaa?

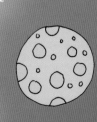

Nitroglycerine

Italian chemist Ascanio Sobrero discovered a powerful new liquid explosive that was so unstable it exploded simply by shaking it. The first "high explosive", nitroglycerine was soon being used for mining and blasting through mountains to build railways. The trouble was, it was so dangerous it was likely to blow up the user.

Dynamite and gelignite

Having blown up his factory for the second time, Swedish explosives manufacturer Alfred Nobel decided to develop a more stable explosive. So he developed a way of solidifying nitroglycerine to make it safe, and named his invention dynamite. Nobel followed this up eight years later with an explosive jelly called gelignite.

Grenades

The first bombs were hand-thrown grenades, comprising hollow balls filled with gunpowder and fitted with a primitive fuse. During World War I, Australian soldiers made their own grenades out of jam tins and gunpowder, giving rise to the term "jam bombs".

Torpedo

Early torpedoes were simply explosives attached to the end of a wooden spar, used for ramming into enemy ships. Asked to improve the design, British engineer Robert Whitehead built the first self-propelled torpedo. Nick-named the Devil's Choice, it was powered by compressed air and had a range of 300m (980ft).

Man o' war

Cannons were used on ships almost as soon as they were invented, but it wasn't until the early 16th century that warships with specially designed gunports were built to carry heavy guns. Launched in 1510, Henry VIII of England's *Mary Rose* was one of the first such warships, powered by sail and armed with 78 guns.

Early submarine

One of the earliest submarines, and the first to carry out an underwater attack, was the pedal-powered *Turtle*, designed by David Bushnell during the American War of Independence. But on its first mission, after struggling for half an hour to attach a mine to the hull of an enemy ship, its pilot simply gave up and fled.

Holland submarine

Early torpedoes were fired from specially designed surface boats, but it was submarines that were to make torpedoes really effective. The first successful submarine was the whale-shaped *Holland VI*, built by Irish-American John Philip Holland. Powered by petrol engine on the surface and by battery underwater, it went into service with the US Navy in 1900.

Bow and arrow

Cave paintings thousands of years old show people hunting with bows and arrows. Such weapons had a longer range than spears, which made them safer for hunting ferocious beasts. Later, bows and arrows became useful as weapons of war.

Ready... Aim... Fire!

c30,000BC

c400BC

Explosive fun! Yay!

c1200

Crossbow

The Chinese invented the first mechanical device for pulling back the string of a bow to increase the projectile power of an arrow. Their new weapon was the crossbow. More deadly than a bow and arrow, it had the disadvantage of taking longer to reload, leaving the user vulnerable to attack.

Don't cross me!

Rocket power

The Chinese invented fireworks around AD1000, using gunpowder to make loud bangs and bursts of flame. Within 200 years they had developed the first rocket fireworks, later adapting them for military use by attaching explosive charges.

Catapult

Like bows and arrows, catapults work using the tension of a tightly stretched drawstring or rope. Greek engineers built the first catapults, but soon the Romans were using them to hurl darts or boulders at the enemy in battle or siege warfare. Huge catapults called ballista were capable of hurling rocks weighing 20kg (44lb) over 350m (1,148ft).

c400BC

Whooaaa! Aaaargh!

Eeeeek

Off with a bang!

Following the invention of gunpowder, weapons relying on tension were slowly phased out in favour of cannons. As these and their successors – the big guns – became more sophisticated, people found novel ways of using them, building heavily armed warships and land vehicles. Torpedoes, bombs, and high explosives also demanded new forms of delivery, giving rise to submarines, fighting aircraft, and rockets. Then the Americans invented the atomic bomb – the most terrifying weapon of them all.

2000BC

You're a menace

c1320

Cannon

Early cannons were built in a similar way to beer barrels, with iron staves held in place by iron hoops. This made them dangerous weapons in more ways than one, as likely to blow up in the user's face as damage enemy fortifications.

War chariot

Four-wheeled battlewagons were developed in Mesopotamia (now modern Iraq) from oxcarts, but they were very clumsy. Switching from four to two wheels, lightening the construction, and replacing oxen with horses resulted in a more mobile and menacing machine – the war chariot.

c600BC

Trireme

The Minoans of Crete built the first navy more than 4,000 years ago, but it was the Greeks who built the first truly impressive warships. Called triremes, they had three banks of oars and were capable of reaching speeds of over eight knots.

POWDER POWER

Var and weapons have been around since the Stone Age, when men first fought over land and food using crude stone implements. By Roman times, the most sophisticated weapons – such as crossbows and catapults – relied on tension to hurl missiles at the enemy. Then the Chinese invented gunpowder. The impact wasn't immediate, and it was nearly 400 years before gunpowder was used to project missiles in battle. But the outcome was to change the scale of warfare for ever.

I can fly!

Gunpowder

About AD900, the Chinese discovered that combining saltpetre (potassium nitrate) with charcoal and sulphur produced an explosive compound, since known as gunpowder. At first they used it to make loud bangs – for entertainment or to scare the enemy – only later using it for rockets and bamboo cannons. By the 14th century, Europeans had discovered the recipe and were employing gunpowder to devastating effect.

Let's get out of here!

Waaheeyyy!

See anything?

Hmmmfff!!

Cannon fire

No-one knows if it was the Chinese, the Arabs, or the Hindus who first discovered that a charge of gunpowder, packed into the closed end of a tube, could explode with enough force to project a missile. Certainly, by the 1320s, the first crude cannons were being employed by the English in warfare. And by the mid-15th century, giant siege cannons were on the scene, capable of firing massive iron balls weighing up to 680kg (1,500lb)!

Shooting Range

Not much good in the rain!

c1350   c1450   c1530   17th century   1814

Missed!

Hand cannon

Not long after the invention of the cannon, the first small firearms, or guns, appeared. Little more than miniature cannons, they were fired by applying a burning coal or hot wire to a touch-hole on the side of the barrel. This ignited the main charge, which exploded and shot the ball out of the gun.

Matchlock musket

By 1450, firearms had acquired triggers and an improved firing mechanism. The matchlock musket had an iron clasp (the lock) that held a smouldering wick (the match). Pulling the trigger swivelled the lock downwards, neatly bringing the match into contact with the gunpowder.

Wheel-lock pistol

The first handguns, or pistols, had a new kind of mechanism that did away with the need for a burning match. Called a wheel-lock, it comprised a serrated wheel that rotated, when the trigger was pulled, against a piece of iron pyrites. This produced a spark to ignite the powder.

Flintlock musket

Probably developed in France in the early 17th century, the flintlock was the simplest, cheapest, and most reliable of all early firing mechanisms, which explains why it held sway for more than 200 years. Even so, at its fastest a flintlock musket could only fire three rounds, or shots, per minute.

Percussion gun

Most early guns were loaded via the muzzle, but all that changed with the invention of the percussion gun. The first models had an external "cap" that, when struck, exploded down a tube into the barrel. Later, the cap was incorporated into a cartridge, along with the main charge and bullet, and loaded directly into the breech.

Flintlock firepower

The key to effective firepower was finding the most efficient means of igniting the charge. The flintlock provided just such a means. To fire a gun, a marksman poured a quantity of gunpowder (called the charge) down the barrel, then rammed a ball down after it using a ramrod. Next, he poured a small amount of gunpowder (the primer) into the priming pan, closed the cover, and pulled the lock back to "full cock". Finally, he took aim and pulled the trigger!

How a flintlock works

Pulling the trigger causes the lock to rotate downwards, scraping a piece of flint against a roughened steel plate (see 2). The friction creates a spark that ignites the primer in the pan, causing a tiny explosion (see 3). This in turn lights the main charge inside the barrel, firing the gun.

1. — Lock
   — Flint
   — Steel

2. Flint scrapes down steel, opening the pan cover
   Primer in the pan

3. A work of friction!
   Primer ignites

Pivoted lock
Priming pan
Flint
Steel
Pan cover
Muzzle (open end of barrel)
Ramrod
Barrel
Breech-firing chamber
Trigger guard
Trigger
Butt or grip

I think we're in trouble!

Did someone shout "duck"?

1867

1836

1862

1884

You're fired!

1919

Get down!

A new alternative

In 1805, bothered by the way birds were alerted by the flash of his gun as the primer ignited, Scottish clergyman and keen duck-hunter Alexander Forsyth designed a new kind of firing mechanism. He replaced the flintlock with a chemical compound that ignited without a spark when struck by a trigger-operated hammer. A turning point in gun design, "percussion" guns soon replaced flintlocks.

Revolver

Percussion firing made multishot guns practical. US inventor Samuel Colt designed the first reliable single-barrelled repeating pistol, with a revolving drum containing five bullet chambers. Before long, his mass-produced revolvers had become the indispensable weapons of the Wild West.

Gatling gun

In 1862, American inventor Richard Gatling built the first practical rapid-fire machine gun, with multiple barrels arranged around a revolving frame. Despite being operated by hand-crank, the Gatling gun was capable of firing up to 1,200 rounds per minute and was soon adopted by the US Army.

Bolt-action rifle

The first reliable multishot rifle was developed by German firearms inventor Paul Mauser. Fitted with a magazine (case) containing five metal cartridges, it was manually operated using a bolt mechanism that, in two swift actions, ejected a spent cartridge from the breech and reloaded a fresh one.

Automatic machine gun

Having invented an automatic mousetrap, US engineer Hiram Maxim went on to invent the automatic machine gun. With a single barrel, and capable of firing over 600 rounds per minute, his gun used the recoil from the exploding charge to eject the spent cartridge and reload a new one.

Thompson submachine gun

US General John Thompson designed the world's first hand-held machine gun. Called the Thompson submachine gun, or "Tommy" gun, it worked on the principle of "blowback", using gas pressure from the exploding charge to eject and reload the cartridges. Soon, gangsters across America were toting Tommy guns!

This thing's going ballistic

ICBMs

During the 1950s, the USSR and the USA raced to build the first ICBM (Intercontinental Ballistic Missile) – that is, a nuclear-armed rocket capable of reaching a distant continent. After several failed attempts, the Russian team, led by Sergei Korolev, successfully launched its multistage R-7, which covered an astonishing 6,400km (4,000 miles).

Saturn V

The success of the R-7 heralded the dawn of a new race – the space race – that reached its peak when the USA landed the first man on the Moon. To make this possible, NASA developed the Saturn V rocket to blast its three-manned Apollo craft into space. The height of a 33-storey building, Saturn V was the most powerful rocket to date.

We have lift off!

1969

Just more stuff to dust

The wages of war

Terrible though war is, the technology developed to wage war has given us many everyday things that we take for granted. Synthetic rubber, tinned food, aviation navigation systems, computers, and the Internet are all the result of military invention. Similarly, bar codes, ready-made meals, and athletic footwear with stay-dry insoles are spin-offs from space technology. .

That thing flies fast

What thing?

1945

1982

Stealth aircraft

Since the advent of radar, enemy aircraft have been easy to detect. Until, that is, the US Air Force introduced the world's first stealth fighter – the F-117 Nighthawk. A combination of special materials and multiangled surfaces makes this aircraft invisible to radar and therefore almost undetectable.

Atomic bomb

Something as innocuously named as *Little Boy* caused the most devastating explosion ever witnessed in warfare. The first atomic bomb used in action, it obliterated the Japanese city of Hiroshima. Developed in the USA by a team of scientists led by Robert Oppenheimer, it heralded the nuclear age, since when people have lived in fear of it ever being used again.

Hmm...

1985

Humvee

Tanks are designed for their firepower, but armies also need fast and reliable vehicles to transport troops, weapons, and cargo into combat. In 1985, the US Army introduced a revolutionary new vehicle that uniquely fitted the bill – the High Mobility Multipurpose Wheeled Vehicle, or HMMWV (pronounced Humvee).

Batteries not included

1954

Nuclear submarine

Battery-powered submarines have to resurface to recharge their batteries. The USS *Nautilus* had no such problem. Its power source was a nuclear reactor, the heat from which created steam to drive a turbine. Without the need to resurface, in 1958 it became the first submarine to sail beneath the polar ice cap and right under the North Pole.

It got away

That's got class

Modular submarine

America's latest range of submarines – the Virginia Class – has a unique modular structure that makes the craft readily upgradable. Individual sections, such as the command centre or weapons module, can be lifted out, modified, and replaced within days, avoiding the need for a lengthy overhaul.

2003

I think I should modify soon

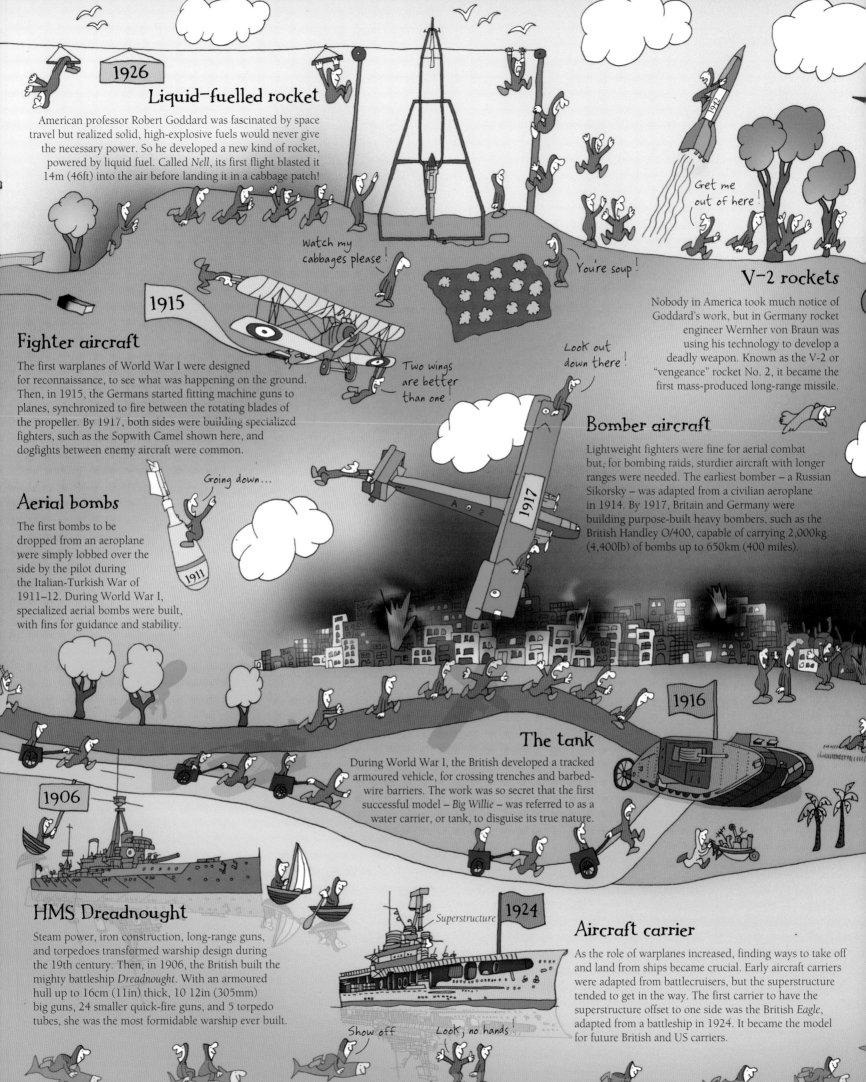

Liquid-fuelled rocket
1926

American professor Robert Goddard was fascinated by space travel but realized solid, high-explosive fuels would never give the necessary power. So he developed a new kind of rocket, powered by liquid fuel. Called *Nell*, its first flight blasted it 14m (46ft) into the air before landing it in a cabbage patch!

Watch my cabbages please!

You're soup!

Get me out of here!

V-2 rockets

Nobody in America took much notice of Goddard's work, but in Germany rocket engineer Wernher von Braun was using his technology to develop a deadly weapon. Known as the V-2 or "vengeance" rocket No. 2, it became the first mass-produced long-range missile.

Fighter aircraft
1915

The first warplanes of World War I were designed for reconnaissance, to see what was happening on the ground. Then, in 1915, the Germans started fitting machine guns to planes, synchronized to fire between the rotating blades of the propeller. By 1917, both sides were building specialized fighters, such as the Sopwith Camel shown here, and dogfights between enemy aircraft were common.

Two wings are better than one!

Look out down there!

Bomber aircraft

Lightweight fighters were fine for aerial combat but, for bombing raids, sturdier aircraft with longer ranges were needed. The earliest bomber – a Russian Sikorsky – was adapted from a civilian aeroplane in 1914. By 1917, Britain and Germany were building purpose-built heavy bombers, such as the British Handley O/400, capable of carrying 2,000kg (4,400lb) of bombs up to 650km (400 miles).

Aerial bombs

The first bombs to be dropped from an aeroplane were simply lobbed over the side by the pilot during the Italian-Turkish War of 1911–12. During World War I, specialized aerial bombs were built, with fins for guidance and stability.

Going down...

The tank
1916

During World War I, the British developed a tracked armoured vehicle, for crossing trenches and barbed-wire barriers. The work was so secret that the first successful model – *Big Willie* – was referred to as a water carrier, or tank, to disguise its true nature.

HMS Dreadnought
1906

Steam power, iron construction, long-range guns, and torpedoes transformed warship design during the 19th century. Then, in 1906, the British built the mighty battleship *Dreadnought*. With an armoured hull up to 16cm (11in) thick, 10 12in (305mm) big guns, 24 smaller quick-fire guns, and 5 torpedo tubes, she was the most formidable warship ever built.

Aircraft carrier
1924

Superstructure

As the role of warplanes increased, finding ways to take off and land from ships became crucial. Early aircraft carriers were adapted from battlecruisers, but the superstructure tended to get in the way. The first carrier to have the superstructure offset to one side was the British *Eagle*, adapted from a battleship in 1924. It became the model for future British and US carriers.

Show off

Look, no hands!

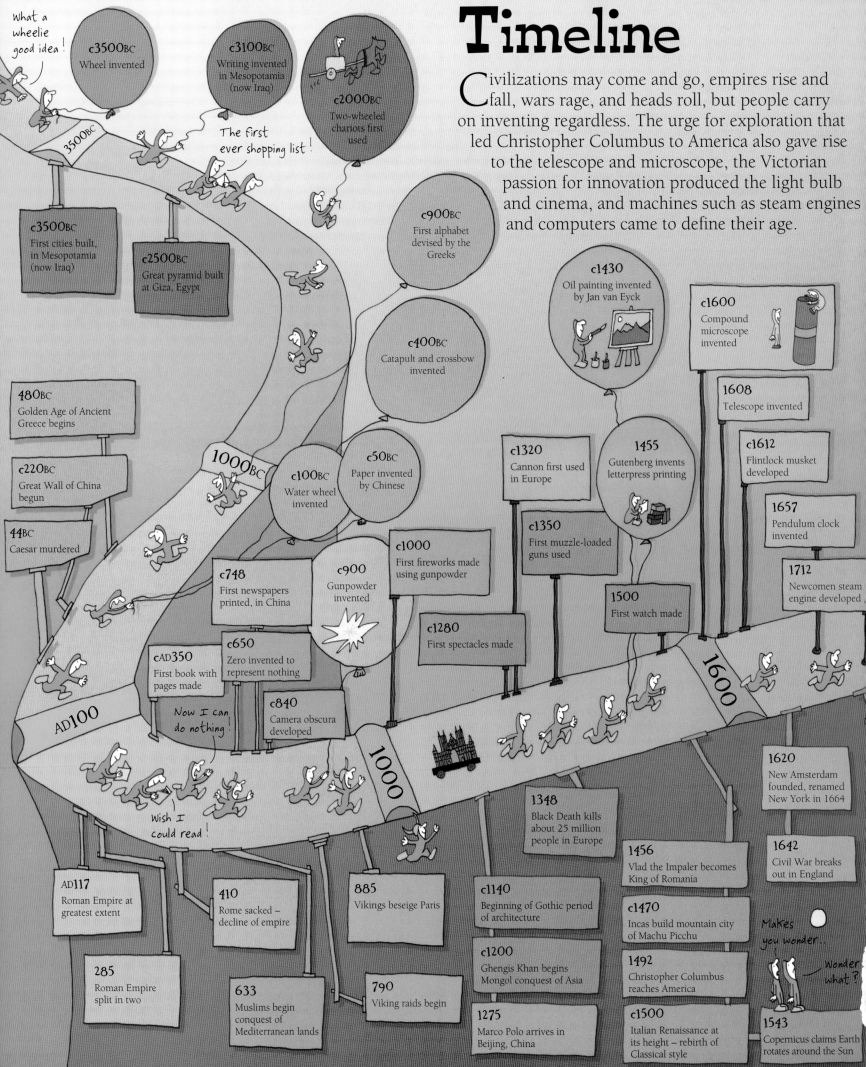

Timeline

Civilizations may come and go, empires rise and fall, wars rage, and heads roll, but people carry on inventing regardless. The urge for exploration that led Christopher Columbus to America also gave rise to the telescope and microscope, the Victorian passion for innovation produced the light bulb and cinema, and machines such as steam engines and computers came to define their age.

What a wheelie good idea!

c3500BC
Wheel invented

c3100BC
Writing invented in Mesopotamia (now Iraq)

The first ever shopping list!

c2000BC
Two-wheeled chariots first used

c900BC
First alphabet devised by the Greeks

c1430
Oil painting invented by Jan van Eyck

c1600
Compound microscope invented

c3500BC
First cities built, in Mesopotamia (now Iraq)

c2500BC
Great pyramid built at Giza, Egypt

c400BC
Catapult and crossbow invented

1608
Telescope invented

480BC
Golden Age of Ancient Greece begins

1000BC

c100BC
Water wheel invented

c50BC
Paper invented by Chinese

c1320
Cannon first used in Europe

1455
Gutenberg invents letterpress printing

c1612
Flintlock musket developed

c220BC
Great Wall of China begun

44BC
Caesar murdered

c1350
First muzzle-loaded guns used

1657
Pendulum clock invented

c1000
First fireworks made using gunpowder

c748
First newspapers printed, in China

c900
Gunpowder invented

1712
Newcomen steam engine developed

1500
First watch made

cAD350
First book with pages made

c650
Zero invented to represent nothing

c1280
First spectacles made

Now I can do nothing!

AD100

c840
Camera obscura developed

Wish I could read!

1600

1348
Black Death kills about 25 million people in Europe

1620
New Amsterdam founded, renamed New York in 1664

1000

AD117
Roman Empire at greatest extent

410
Rome sacked – decline of empire

885
Vikings beseige Paris

c1140
Beginning of Gothic period of architecture

1456
Vlad the Impaler becomes King of Romania

1642
Civil War breaks out in England

c1470
Incas build mountain city of Machu Picchu

Makes you wonder..

285
Roman Empire split in two

633
Muslims begin conquest of Mediterranean lands

790
Viking raids begin

c1200
Ghengis Khan begins Mongol conquest of Asia

1492
Christopher Columbus reaches America

Wonder what?

1275
Marco Polo arrives in Beijing, China

c1500
Italian Renaissance at its height – rebirth of Classical style

1543
Copernicus claims Earth rotates around the Sun

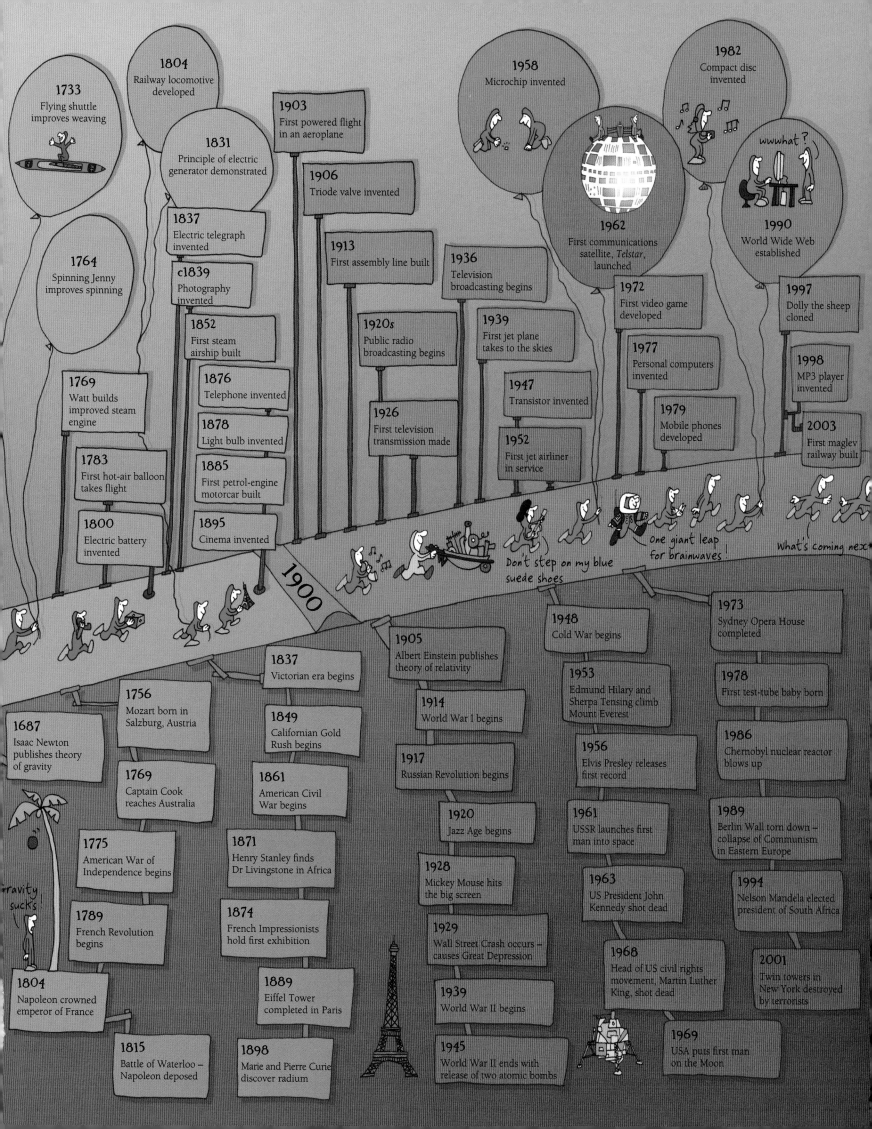

GLOSSARY

3-D
Meaning three-dimensional – that is, something that has depth and volume rather than being flat, or two-dimensional.

Aerodynamics
The mathematical study of the relationship between, usually, air or wind and solid objects such as aeroplanes and buildings. It plays an important part in the design process, helping engineers to achieve the best levels of safety and performance.

Airship
A lighter-than-air craft traditionally comprising a cigar-shaped body containing several helium-filled balloons and usually powered by petrol engine. Unlike balloons, which float wherever the wind takes them, airships are steerable, or "dirigible".

Alternating current
An electrical current that continually changes its direction of flow, flowing first one way, then the other, then back again. Modern power stations supply alternating current.

Arc light
A form of electric light in which an electrical discharge jumps, or arcs, between two carbon rods, creating an intense glow.

Assembly line
A fast way of manufacturing goods, such as cars and washing machines, pioneered by Henry Ford in 1913. Items under construction are carried along a conveyor belt past a line of workers, each of whom repeatedly performs a specific function, such as fitting a door or adding a bumper.

Atomic bomb
A type of bomb that relies on nuclear fission (see entry) to release vast amounts of nuclear energy, so causing a devastating explosion. It was the dropping of two such bombs that brought World War II to an end.

Binary code
A system used in modern computers in which information is stored and tasks carried out using coded sequences of "0"s and "1"s.

Breech
The part of a gun, behind the barrel, that carries the shells or cartridges.

Cat's whisker
Part of a device in early radio sets designed to detect radio signals. It comprised a fine wire that listeners twiddled over a special crystal until they had picked up a signal. Fiddly to operate, it was soon superseded by electronic valves.

Cathode ray
See electron beam entry.

Cloning
Making an identical copy of an organism, such that they have exactly the same genes (units carrying hereditary data).

Concave lens
An inward curved lens that makes distant objects look closer and smaller than they really are.

Convex lens
An outward curved lens that makes objects look bigger and further away than they really are. Convex lenses are used in magnifying glasses.

Current, electric
A flow of electrons through a "conductor", such as a copper wire. (See also: alternating current and direct current entries.)

Cylinder
A tube-shaped chamber containing a piston (see entry), found, for example, in steam and petrol engines. Inside, the piston is driven back and forth to create movement.

Data
The information stored inside a computer.

Direct current
An electric current that flows in one direction only, as opposed to an alternating current, which continually changes direction. Edison's first power stations supplied direct current, but alternating current soon became standard.

Ejector seat
An explosive-propelled safety device used in military aircraft that can blast the occupant free of the craft in an emergency.

Electromagnet
A magnet formed by passing an electric current through a coil of wire surrounding an iron core. The current creates a magnetic field, turning the iron into a magnet for as long as the current flows.

Electron
A negatively-charged particle found in the outer layers of an atom.

Electron beam
A stream of electrons, also known as a cathode ray, used in television sets and electron microscopes.

Electronics
The use of devices in which electricity in one circuit controls electricity in another circuit. For example, in a television set, the electric signal from the aerial controls an electron beam as it moves across the screen to create an image. Modern computers rely on electronic "controlling" devices, such as transistors, to perform their various functions.

Fluorescent lamp
A type of electric lamp that glows when radiation from mercury vapour causes a phosphor coating inside the lamp to glow.

Flying boat
A type of aeroplane that can take off and land on water.

Flying shuttle
An automatic device invented in the 18th century to speed up the weaving process. Operated by fast-moving weights (that acted like hammers), the flying shuttle shot between the warp (vertical) threads at high speed, carrying the weft (horizontal) thread with it. It meant that, when making wide cloth, a single weaver could operate a loom from a fixed position, without needing an assistant to catch the shuttle and throw it back again.

Flywheel
A large heavy wheel designed to smooth out the operation of an engine by preventing sudden changes of speed.

Fossil fuels
Fuels such as coal, oil, and natural gas that derive from rotting organic matter laid down millions of years ago. Burning these fuels to release their energy creates "greenhouse gases" that may be causing global warming (see entry) and damaging our planet.

Gears
Toothed wheels that engage with each other in order to alter the speed or direction of motion within an engine, machine, or vehicle.

Global warming
A process by which our planet may be heating up, causing widespread problems such as floods, droughts, storms, forest fires, and melting ice caps. Many scientists believe burning fossil fuels and creating too many "greenhouse gases" has resulted in global warming.

Greenhouse gases
Gases such as methane, carbon dioxide, and water vapour that create a blanket around the Earth, trapping heat from the sun. This "greenhouse effect" is a natural phenomenon that helps to keep us warm, but we may be upsetting the balance by creating too many greenhouse gases, causing our planet to heat up (see global warming).

Hybrid car
A car with both a petrol engine and an electric motor and that is powered by one or the other according to the speed at which it's travelling.

Hypersonic
Travelling at least five times faster than the speed of sound.

ICBM
Intercontinental Ballistic Missile. A long-range guided missile fired from land or sea to a surface target a great distance away. Nuclear ICBMs are rocket-powered and travel at high speed through the

fringes of space before dropping back down to Earth.

Industrial Revolution
A revolution in the way people lived and worked that started in Britain about 250 years ago before spreading throughout the western world. It was caused by a host of inventions, such as the power loom, that led to the establishment of large factories. Over time, the factories drew people away from working at home or on the land, concentrating them in over-crowded cities.

Internal combustion engine
An engine that burns fuel in a chamber *inside* the engine, rather than *outside* it, as in a steam engine. There are three main types: petrol engines as used in cars and motorbikes; diesel engines used mainly for heavy machinery, lorries and trains; and turbojets, used to power jet aircraft.

Lightning conductor
A spiked metal rod fitted to the top of a building and connected to rods in the ground that protects a building from being damaged by lightning. It works by harmlessly conducting electricity from a lightning strike to the ground rather than allowing it to travel through the building itself.

Microchip
A tiny slice of a special material called a semiconductor (eg, silicon) that incorporates, in miniature, all the components found on a circuit board, made up of separate electronic parts, such as transistors, capacitors, and resistors. The components are an integral part of the semiconductor material, giving the microchip its alternative name of integrated circuit.

Microprocessor
The brain of a computer, combining the functions of many microchips on a single unit and capable of carrying out several billion operations every second. A typical microprocessor chip contains about 50 million transistors. These are so tiny that if you enlarged the chip so that the smallest detail measured 0.1mm (0.004 in) across, the chip would be as tall as a five-storey building!

Microwaves
A type of radiation (energy in wave form), related to visible light and radio waves.

Monoplane
An aeroplane with one set of wings.

Muzzle
The open end of a gun barrel.

Nuclear fission
Splitting the nucleus (central core) of a heavy atom such as uranium to release energy. Modern nuclear power stations use nuclear fission to generate electricity.

Nuclear fusion
Combining two atomic nuclei (cores) of a light element such as deuterium (a form of hydrogen) to release energy. Nuclear fusion provides the explosive power of hydrogen bombs but, one day in the future, it may be put to better use generating electricity.

Patent
A form of legal protection that gives an inventor or organization the sole right to make, use, or sell an invention for a fixed period. It prevents others from profiting from an inventor's ideas. In return, the inventor discloses full details of the invention so that anyone can make it once the patent has expired.

Percussion
Striking one solid material against another, such as in drums and other percussion instruments. In percussion guns, a hammer strikes a small charge of special powder that explodes upon impact, causing the gun to fire.

Piston
A tightly fitting disk that is driven back and forth inside a cylinder to create motion.

Pneumatic tyre
A rubber tyre filled with air, commonly used on bicycles, cars, and aeroplanes. Pneumatic tyres give a far smoother ride than solid rubber tyres.

Program, computer
A set of instructions stored in a computer's memory that tells the computer what sequence of operations to perform.

Radio signal
A radio wave that has information about sound, pictures, or other data superimposed onto it. Radio receivers can pick up the signal via an aerial and convert the superimposed information back into sound.

Radio wave
A type of radiation (energy in wave form), related to light and X-rays. It can be modulated (varied) to carry information about sound or pictures to radios or television sets. In wireless telegraphy, radio waves were emitted as pulses to send coded messages.

Satellite
A body, such as a moon, that orbits the Earth or another planet. Artificial satellites are sent into orbit around the Earth to relay television, radio, and computer data from one side of the globe to the other.

Screw propeller
A screw-shaped propeller used to drive ships through water. It replaced the paddle wheel in the mid-19th century.

Smelting
A way of extracting metals from their ores (mineral compounds containing metals) using heat.

Stethoscope
A medical instrument that enables doctors to listen to sounds inside the body, such as the heart beat.

Supersonic
Travelling faster than the speed of sound – that is, more than 1,240kph at 20°C (770mph at 70°F).

Superstructure
In naval terms, that part of a ship or aircraft carrier that rises up above the main deck and forms the command centre of the vessel.

Switch
In computer terms, an electronic device, such as a transistor or valve, that turns an electric current on or off. In most modern computers that use binary code (see entry), switching the current "off" corresponds to "0" and switching it "on" corresponds to "1".

Telegraphy
A way of transmitting signals or messages over long distances using, for example, flags, radio waves, or pulses of electric current.

Tungsten
A metallic element, commonly used in incandescent light bulbs, that glows for a long time without melting or boiling away.

Ultraviolet light
A type of radiation (energy in wave form) related to visible light and radio waves.

Valve, electronic
A device that looks something like a light bulb and which causes an electric current to flow in one direction only. It also allows the current to be controlled by electricity. Before transistors were invented, different types of valve were widely used to detect radio signals, amplify sound, and act as switches in computers.

Valve, mechanical
A device that controls the flow of liquids or gases through a pipe, either turning the flow on or off, as in a common kitchen tap, or allowing the liquids or gases to flow in one direction only.

X-rays
A type of radiation (energy in wave form) related to visible light and radio waves.

INDEX

Dual-stratified internal steam combusted triode-manipulated barrow-oscillating tea-maker (beta version)

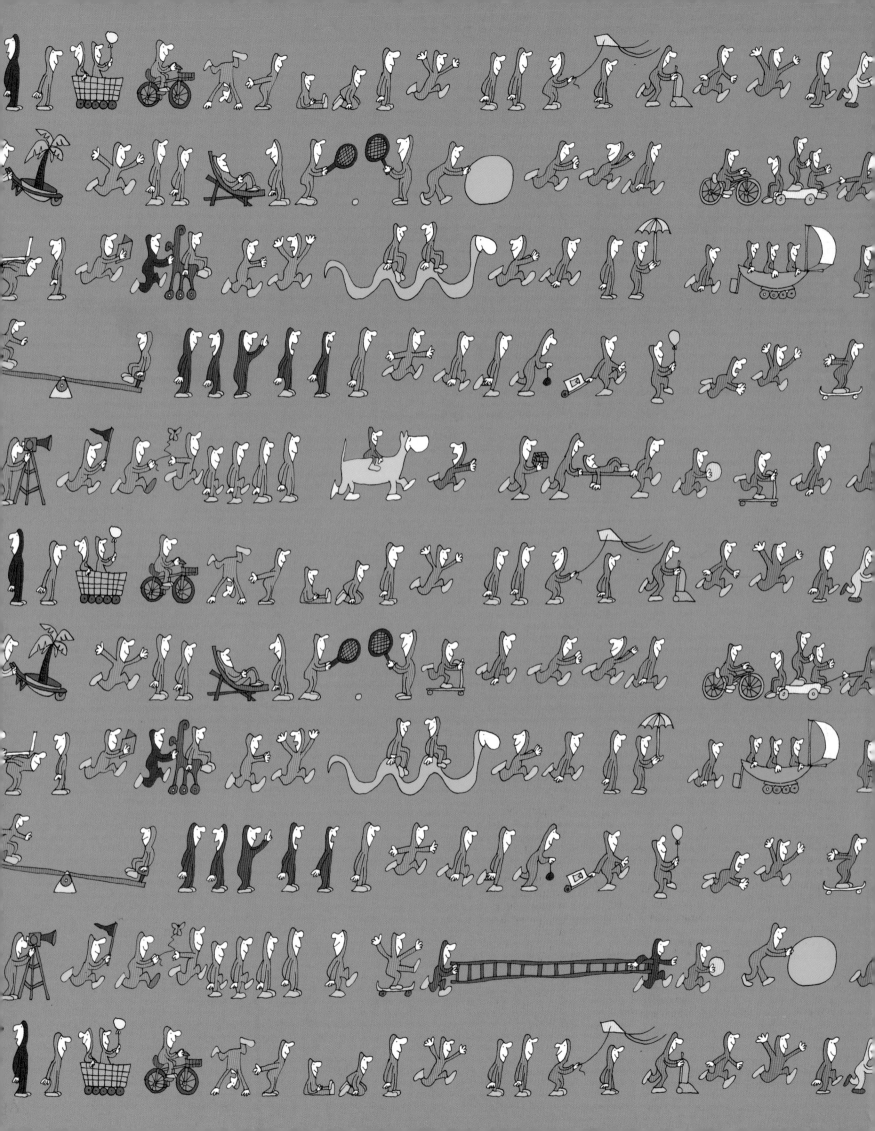